This Book Belongs To:

____

Need a break
from your day?

Take a

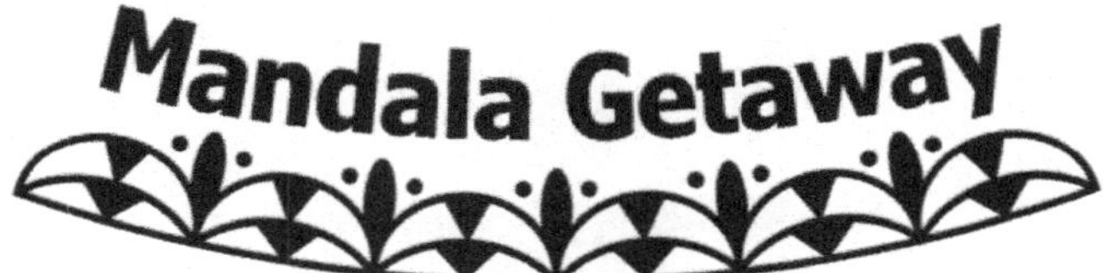

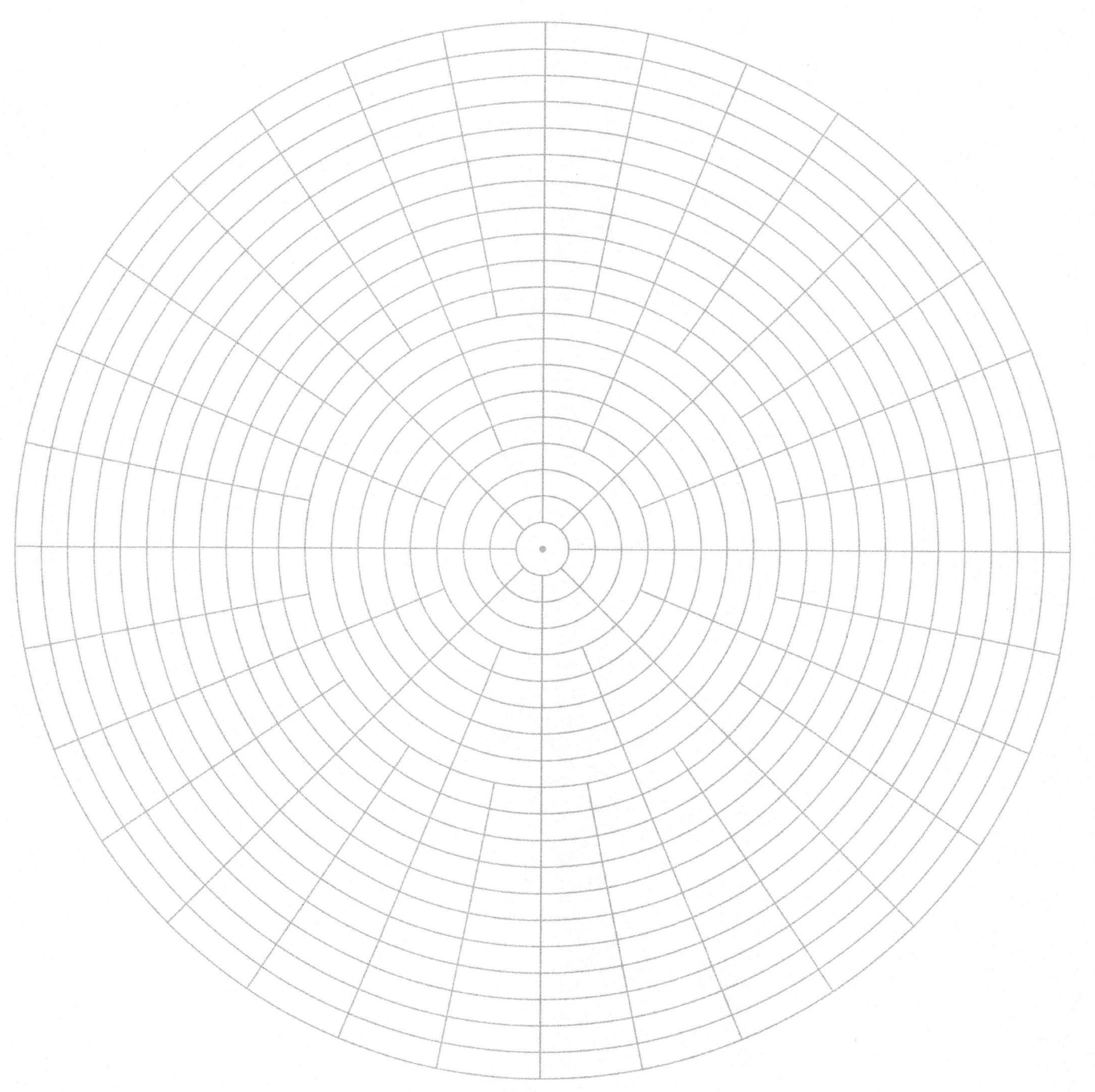

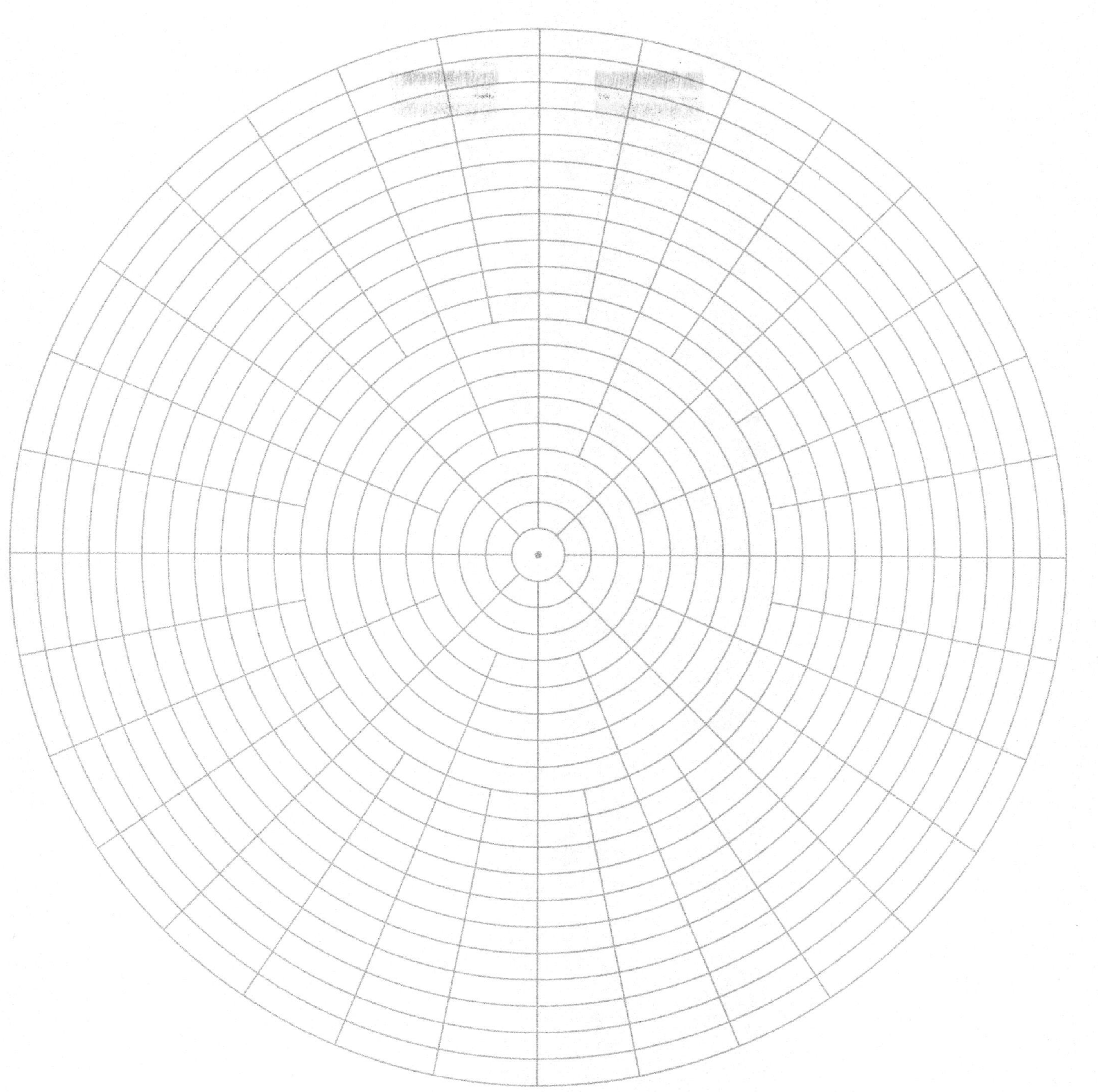

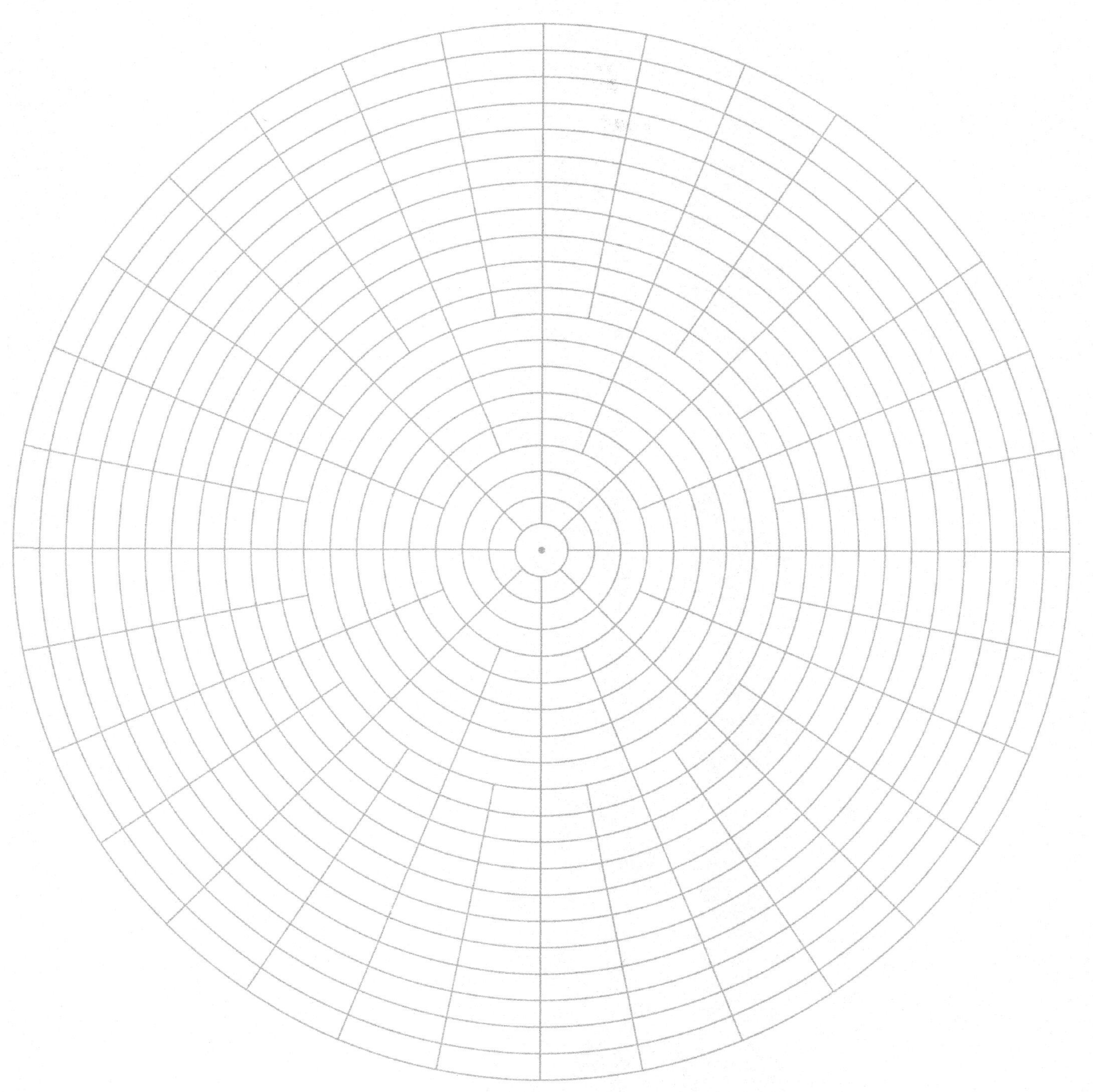

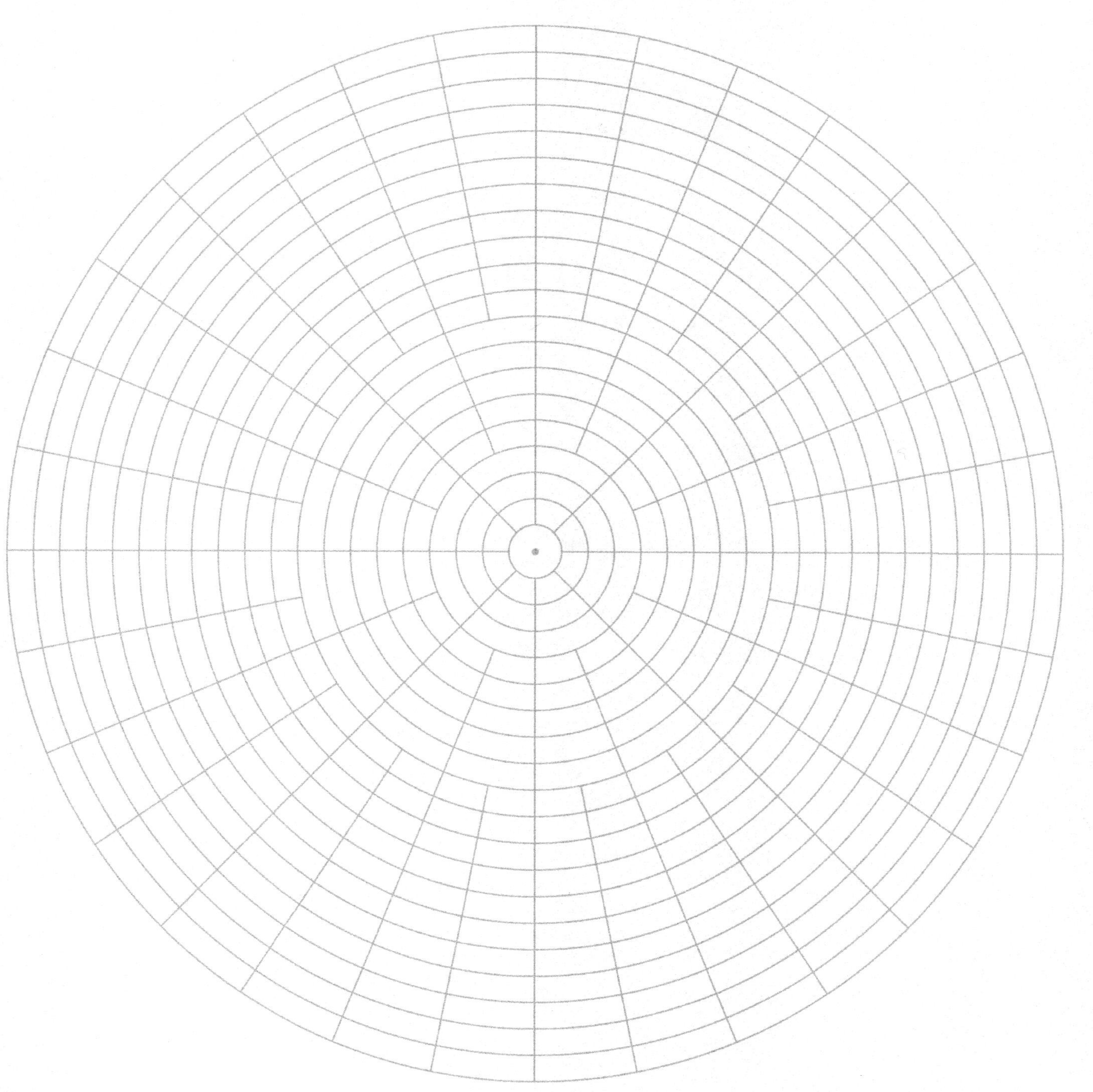

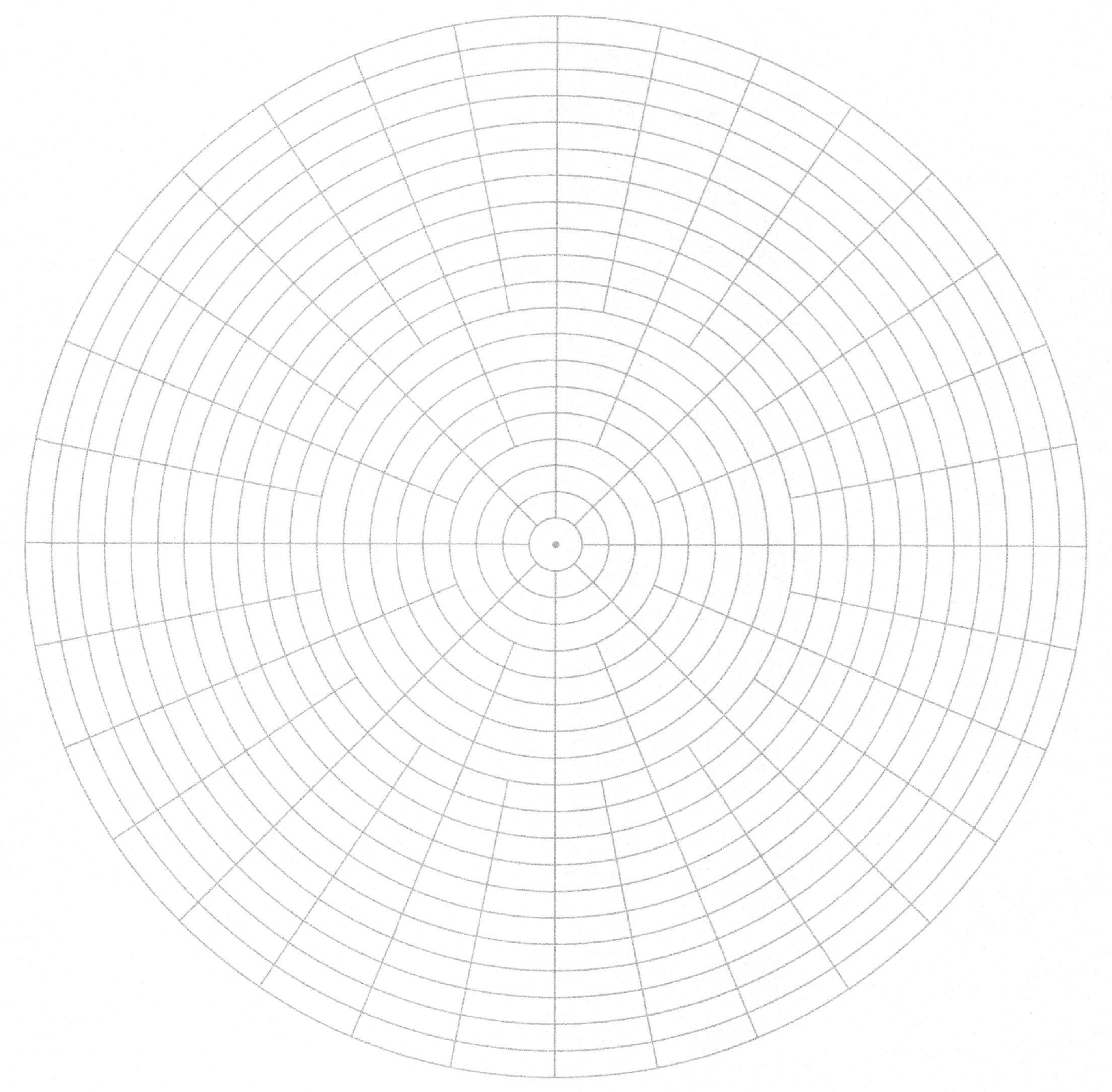

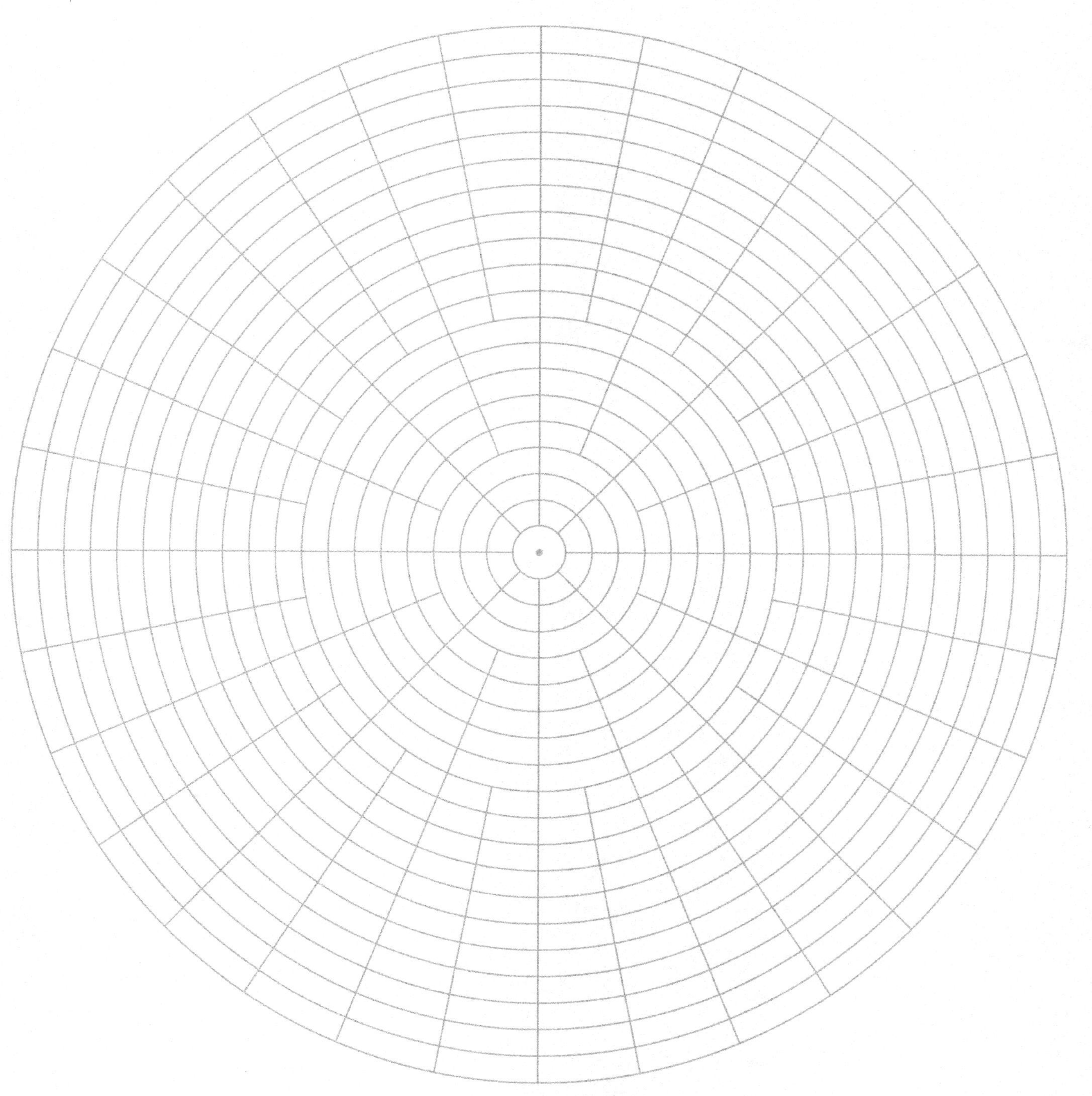

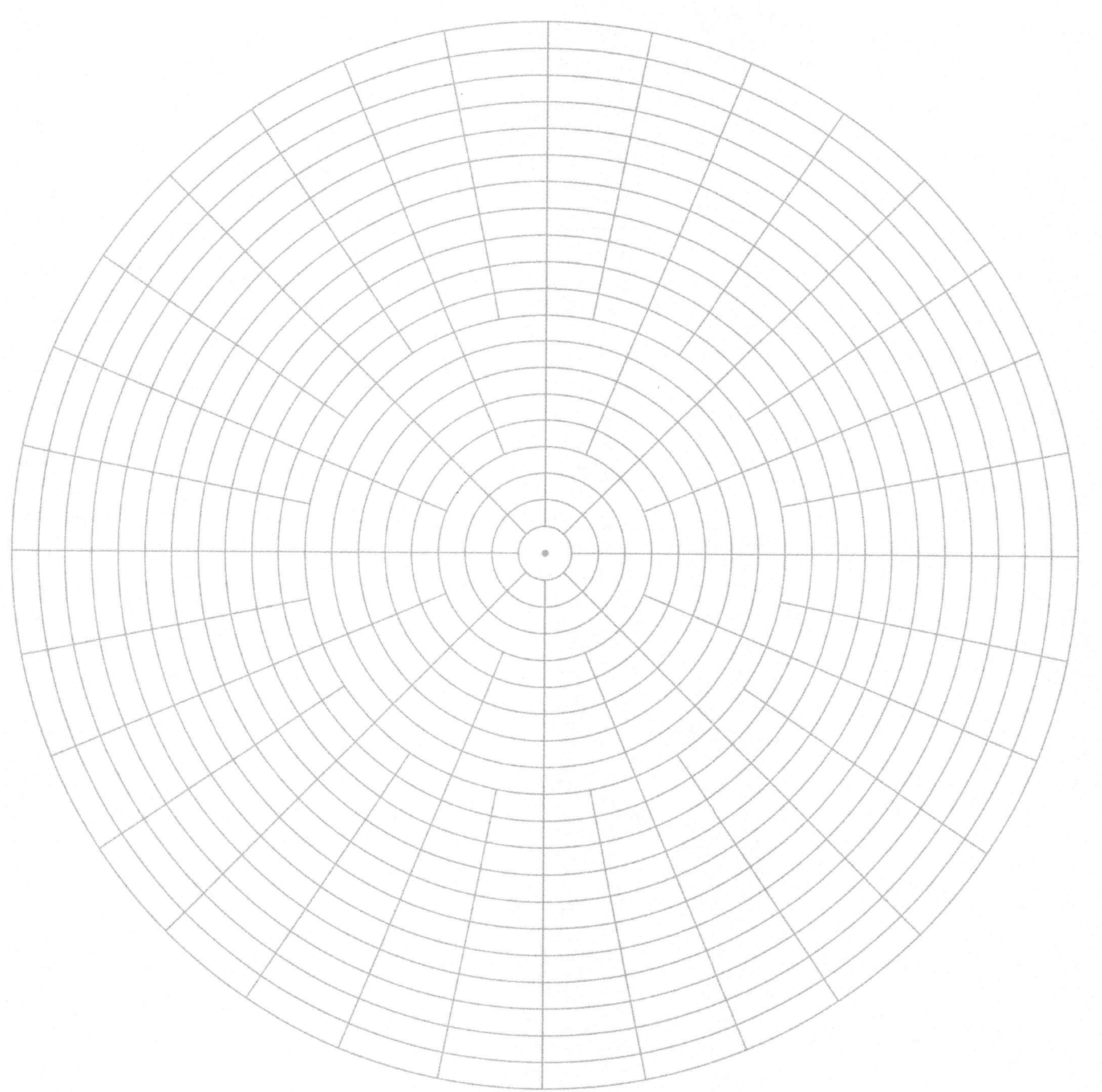

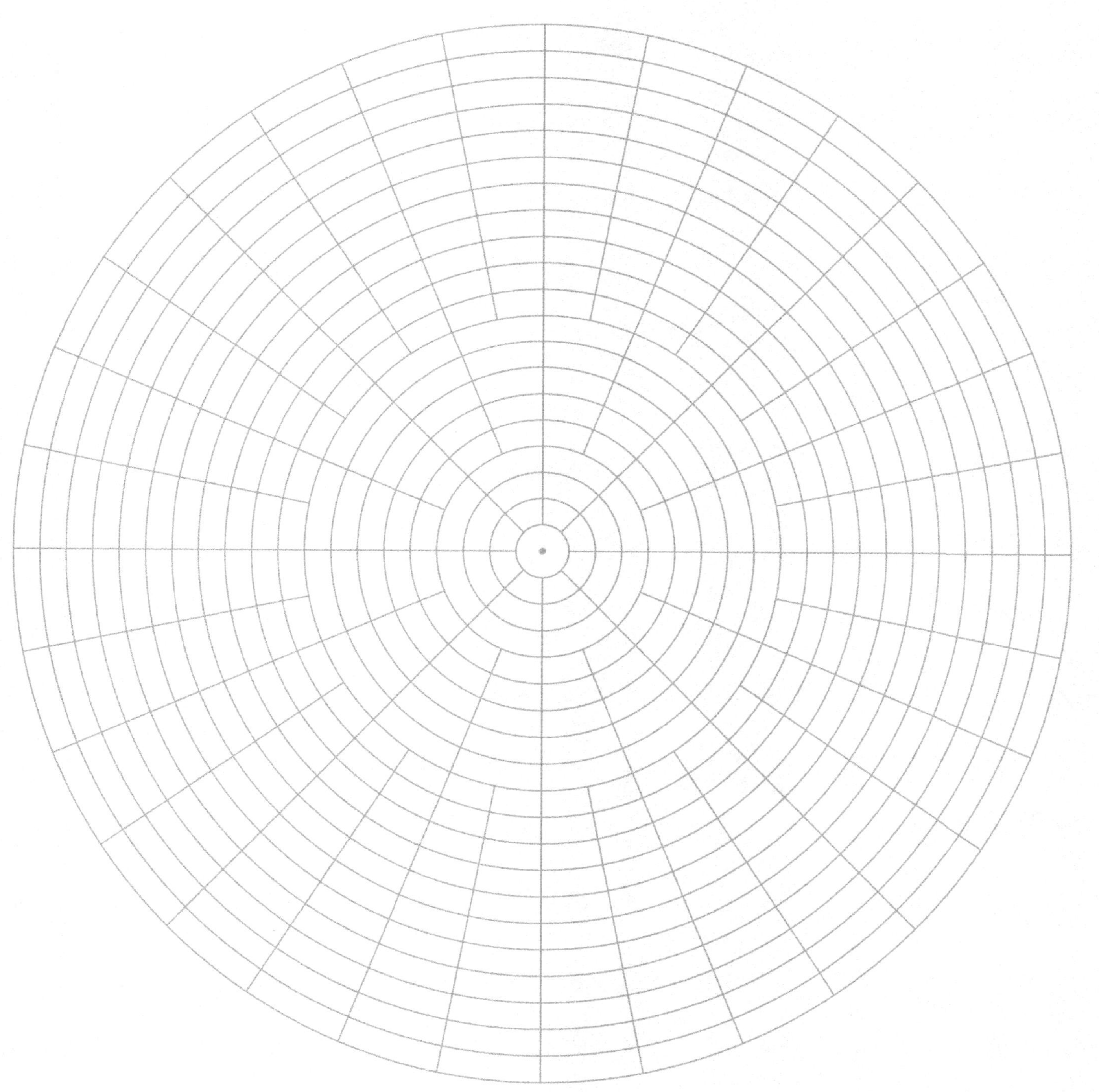

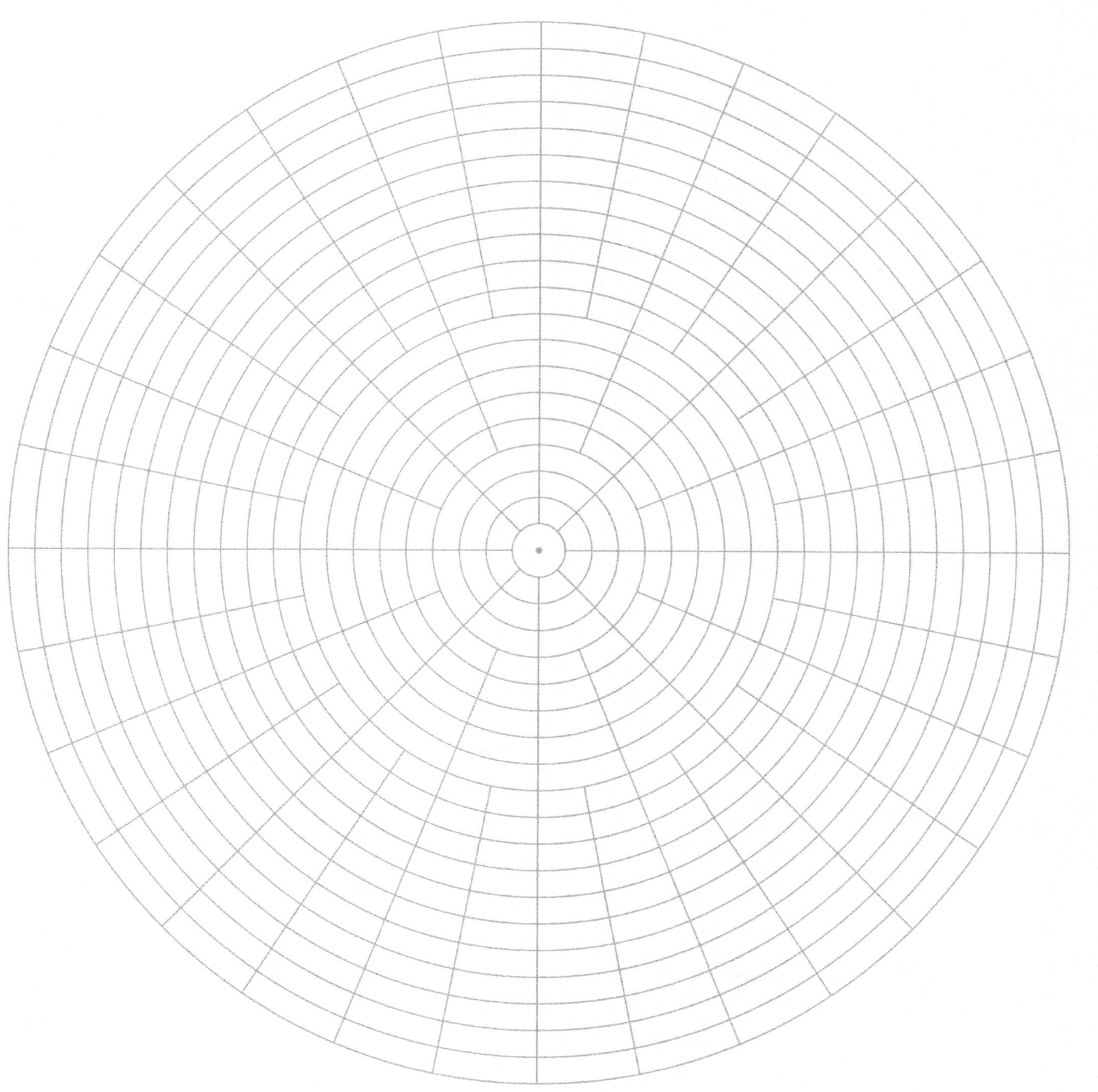

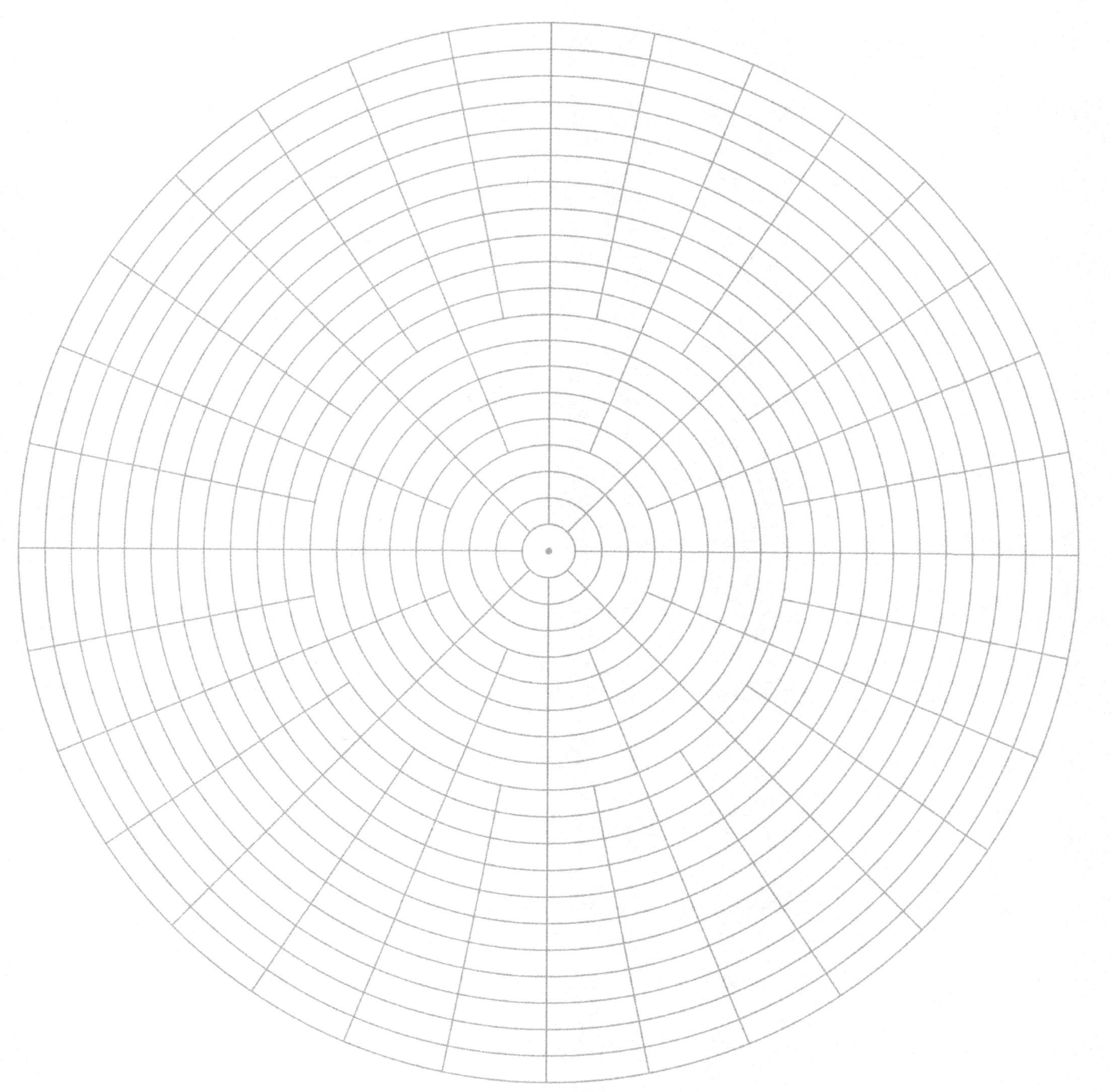

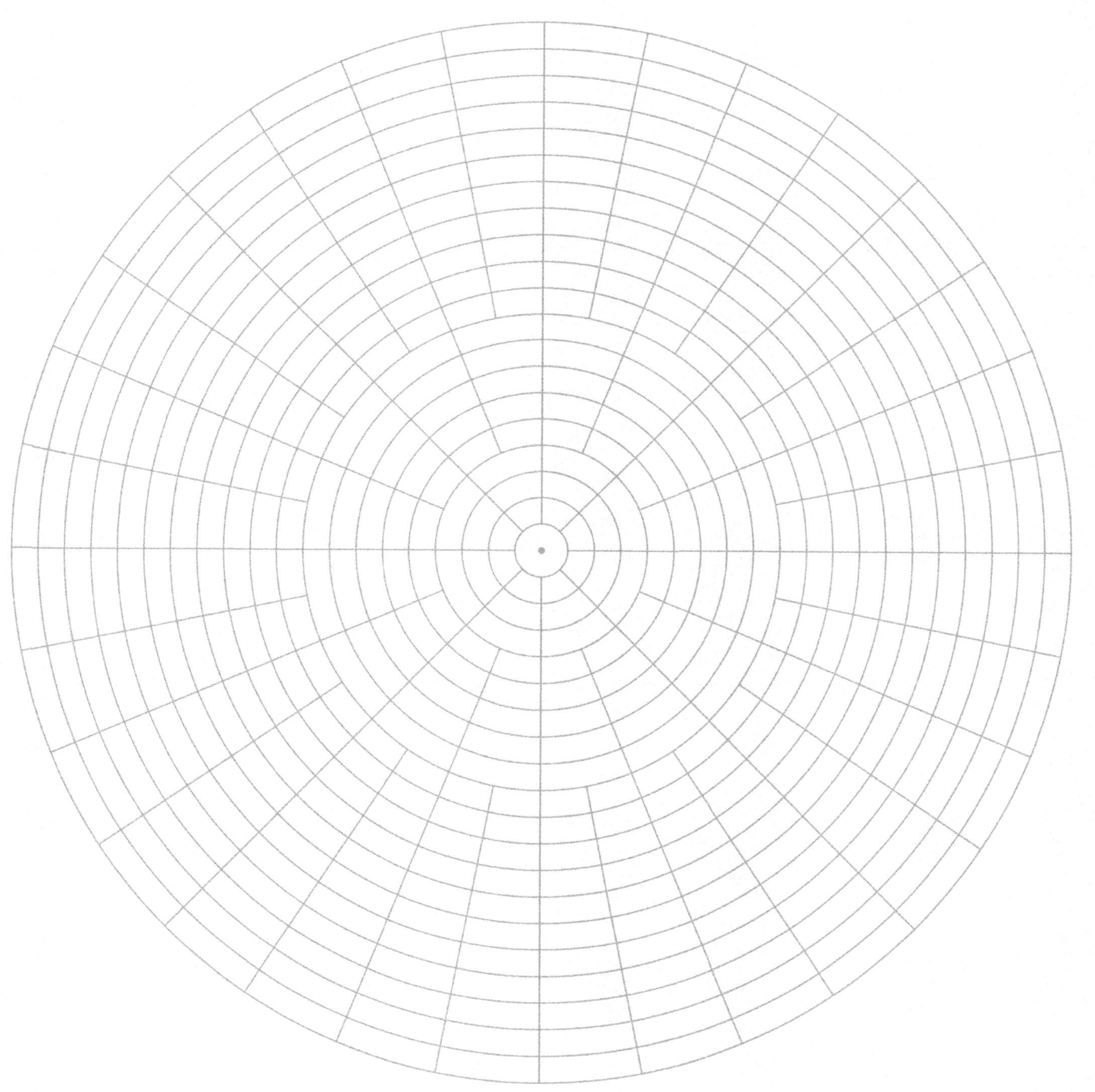

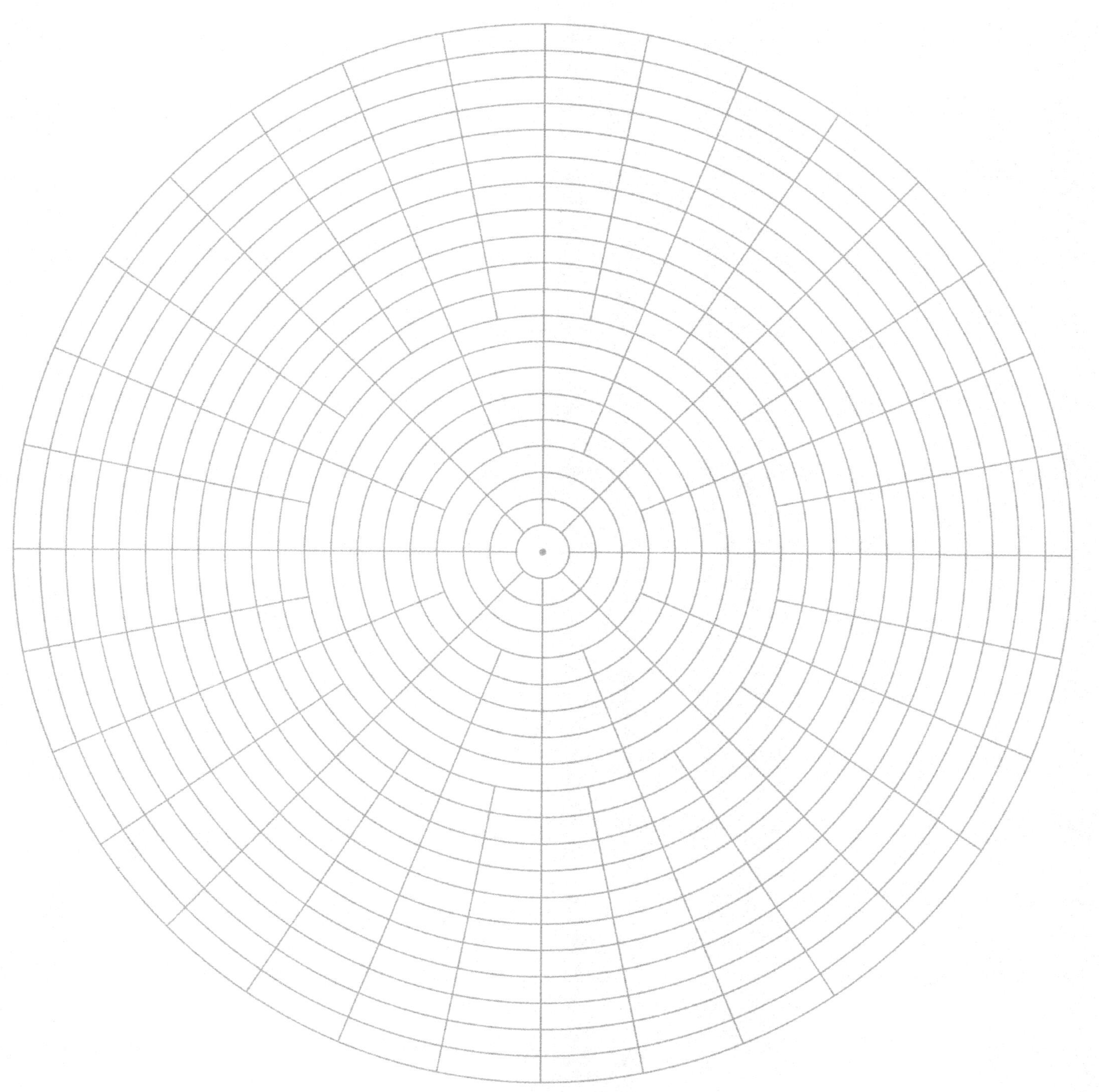

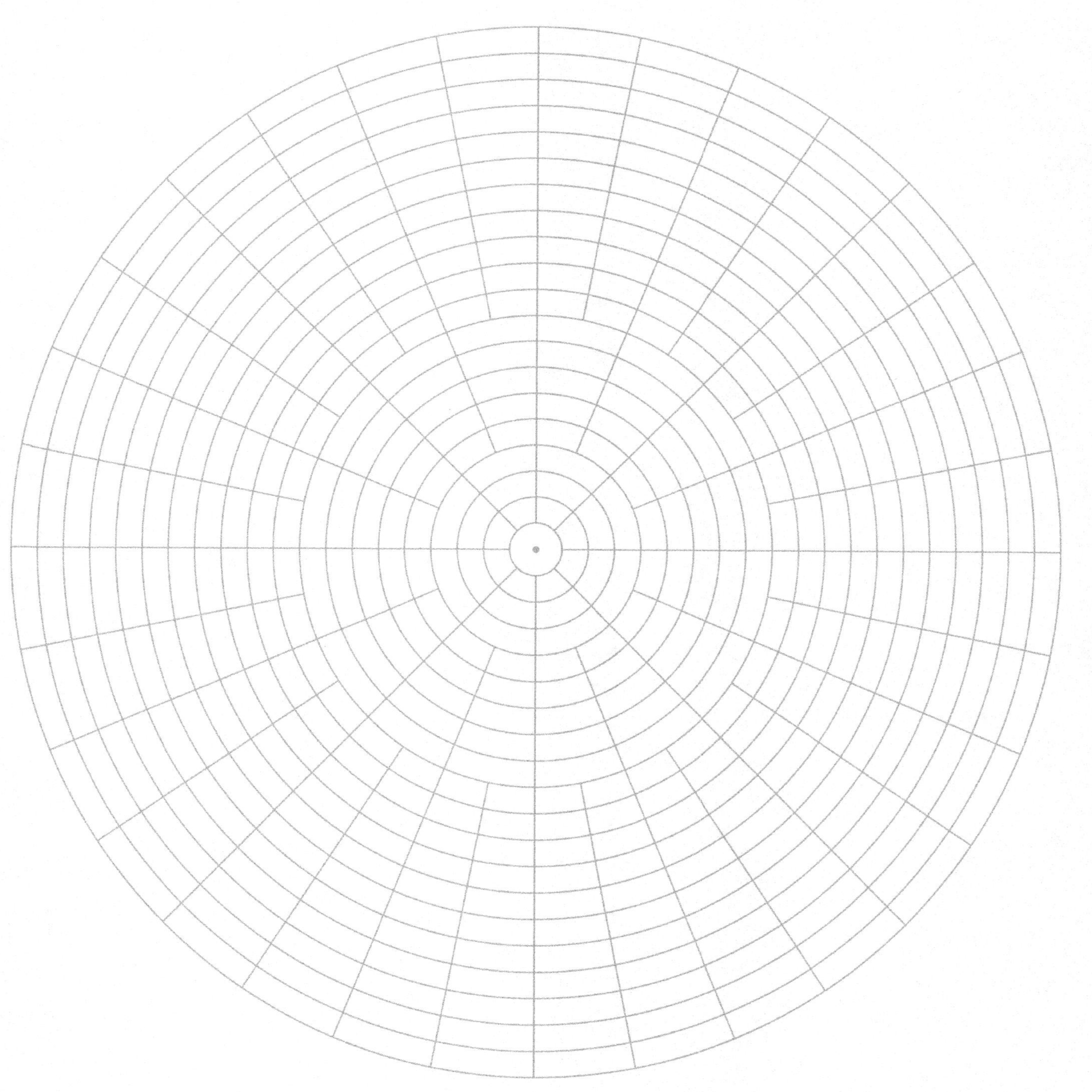

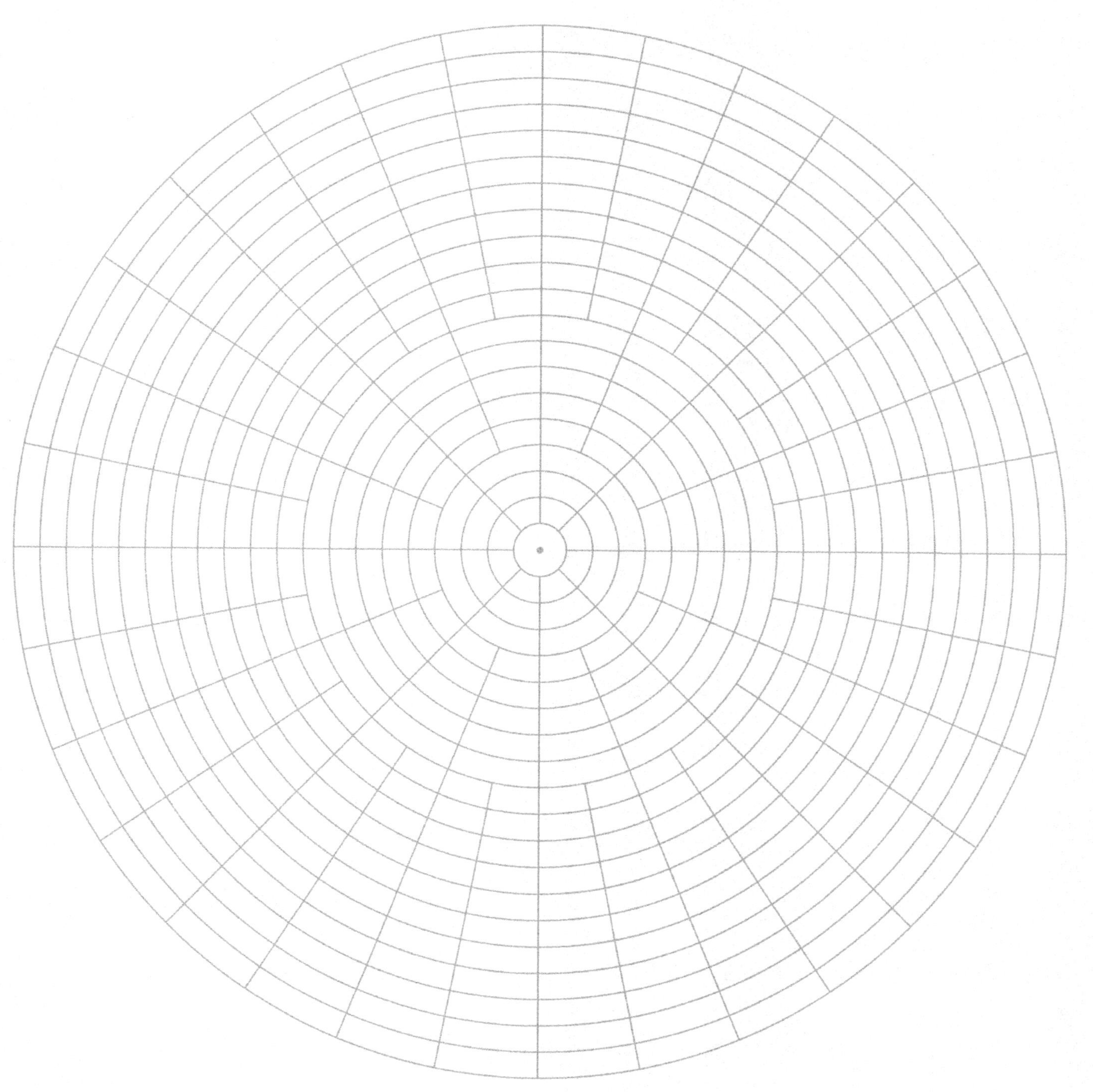

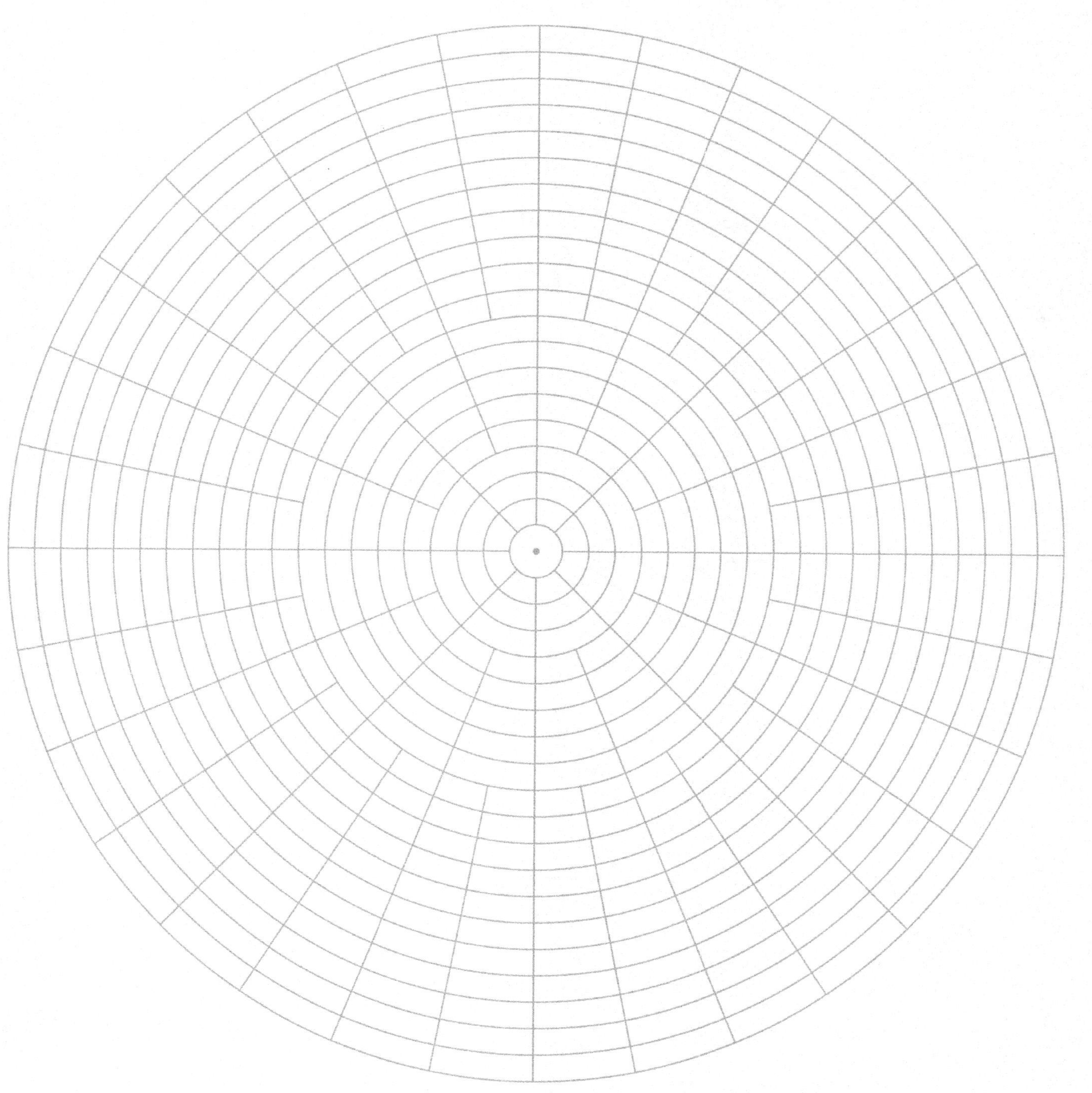

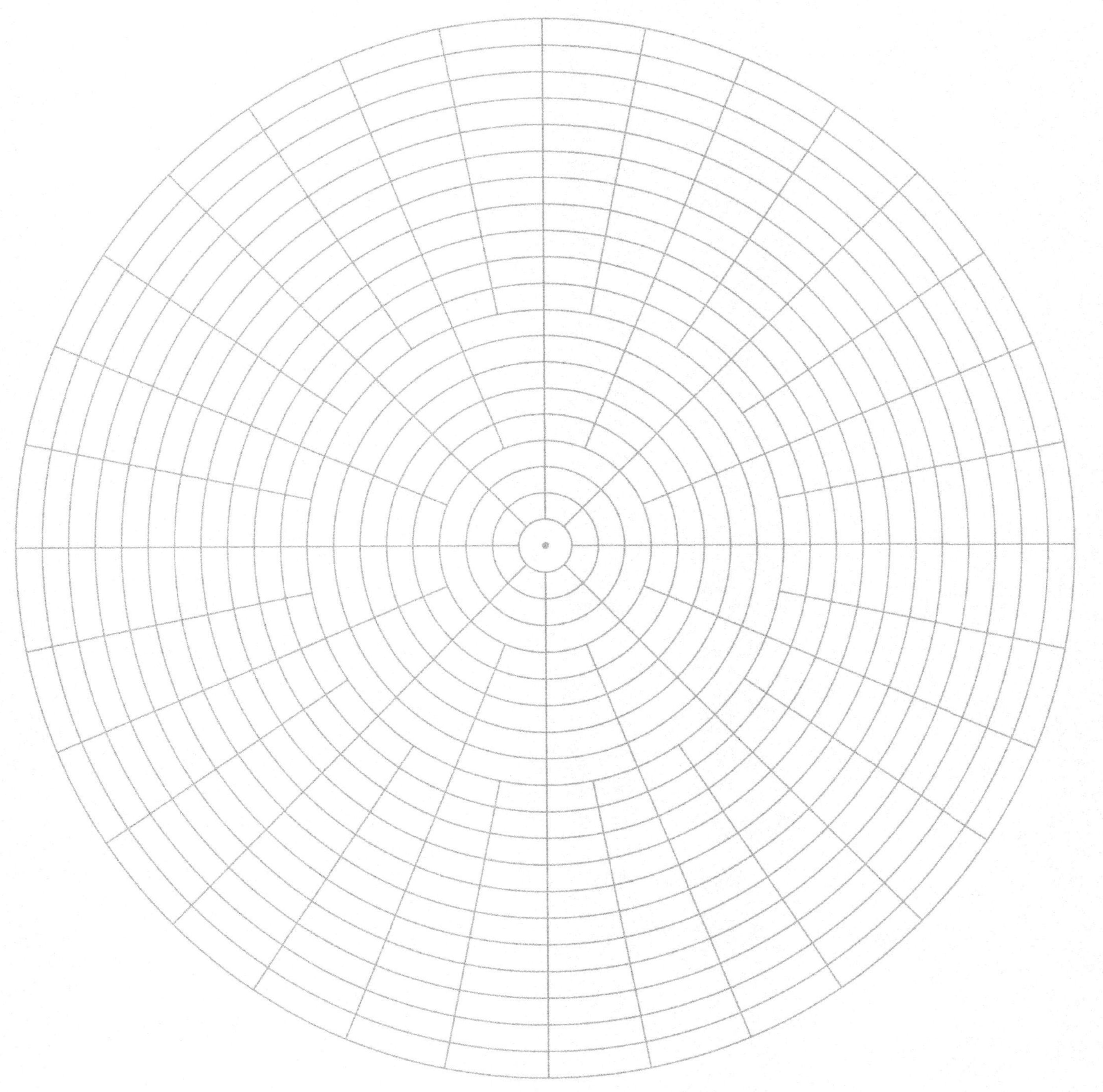

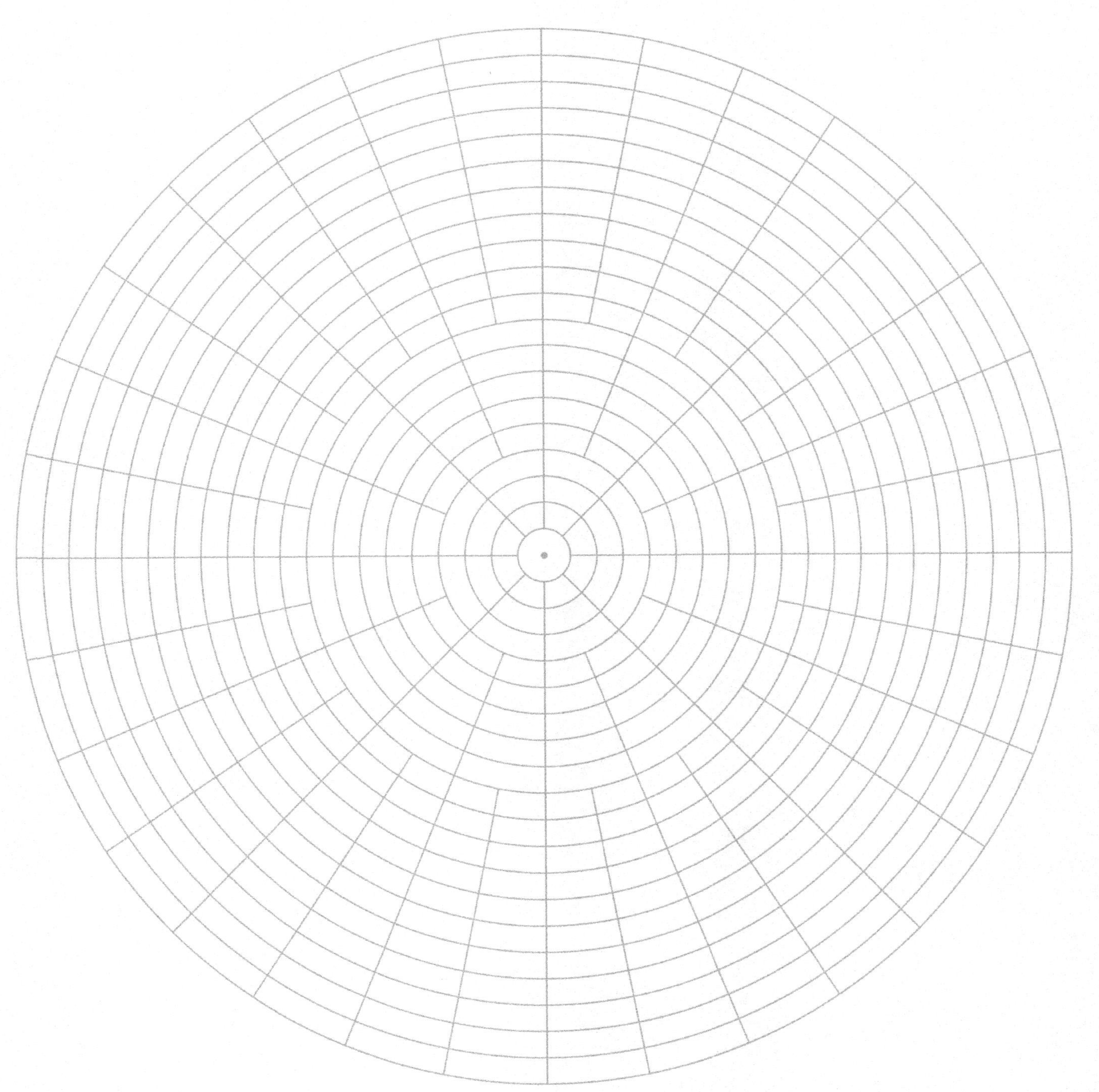

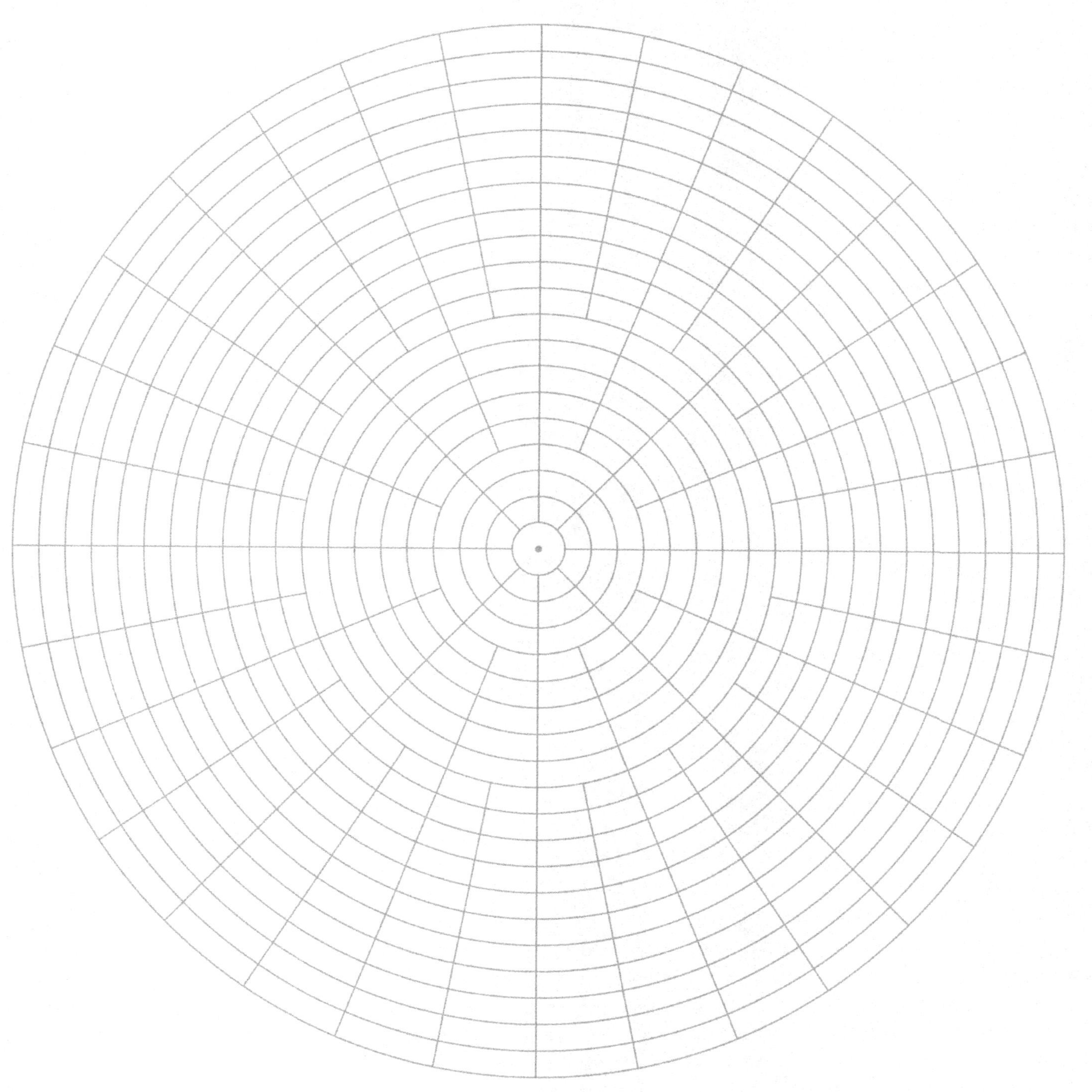

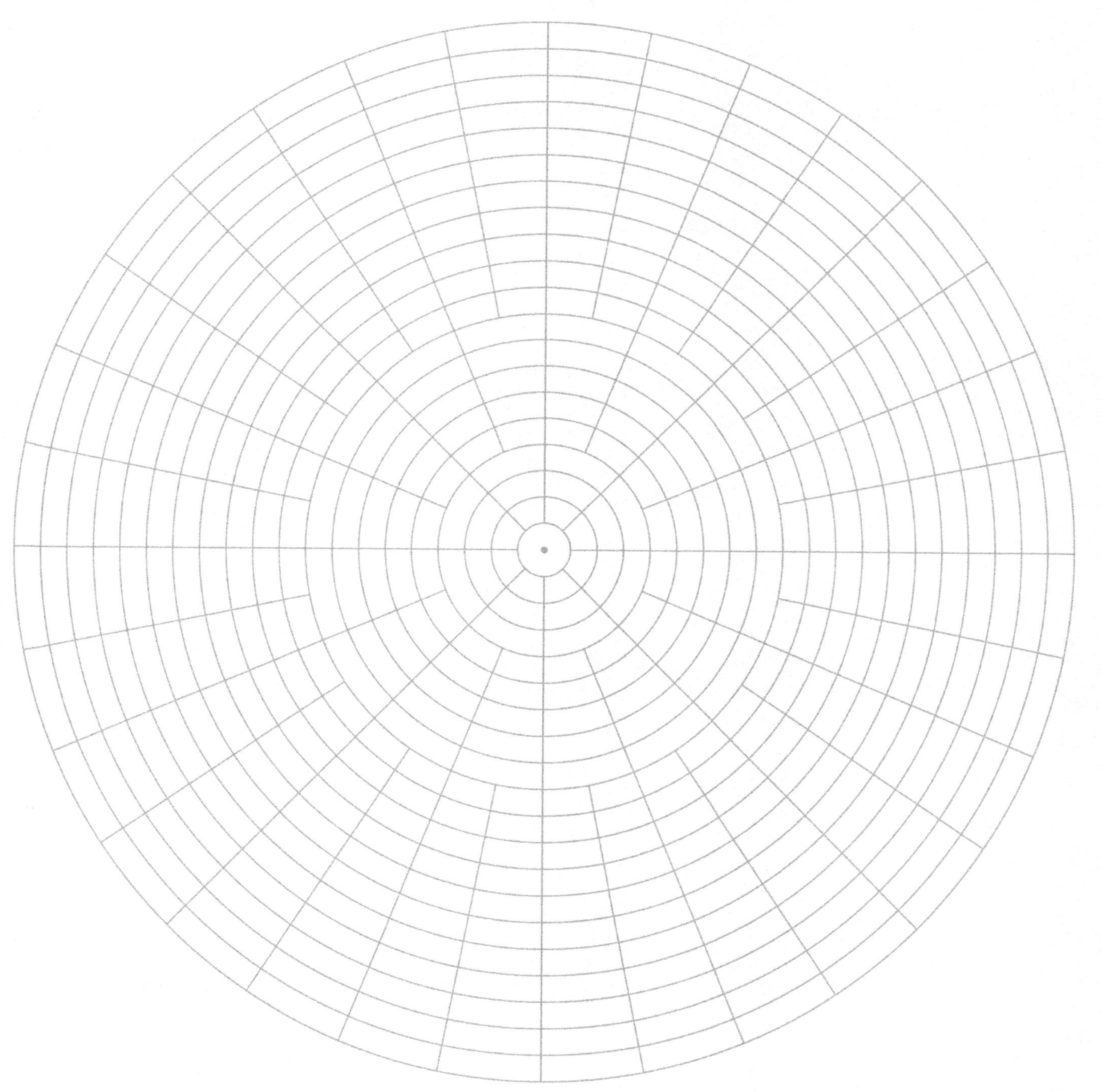

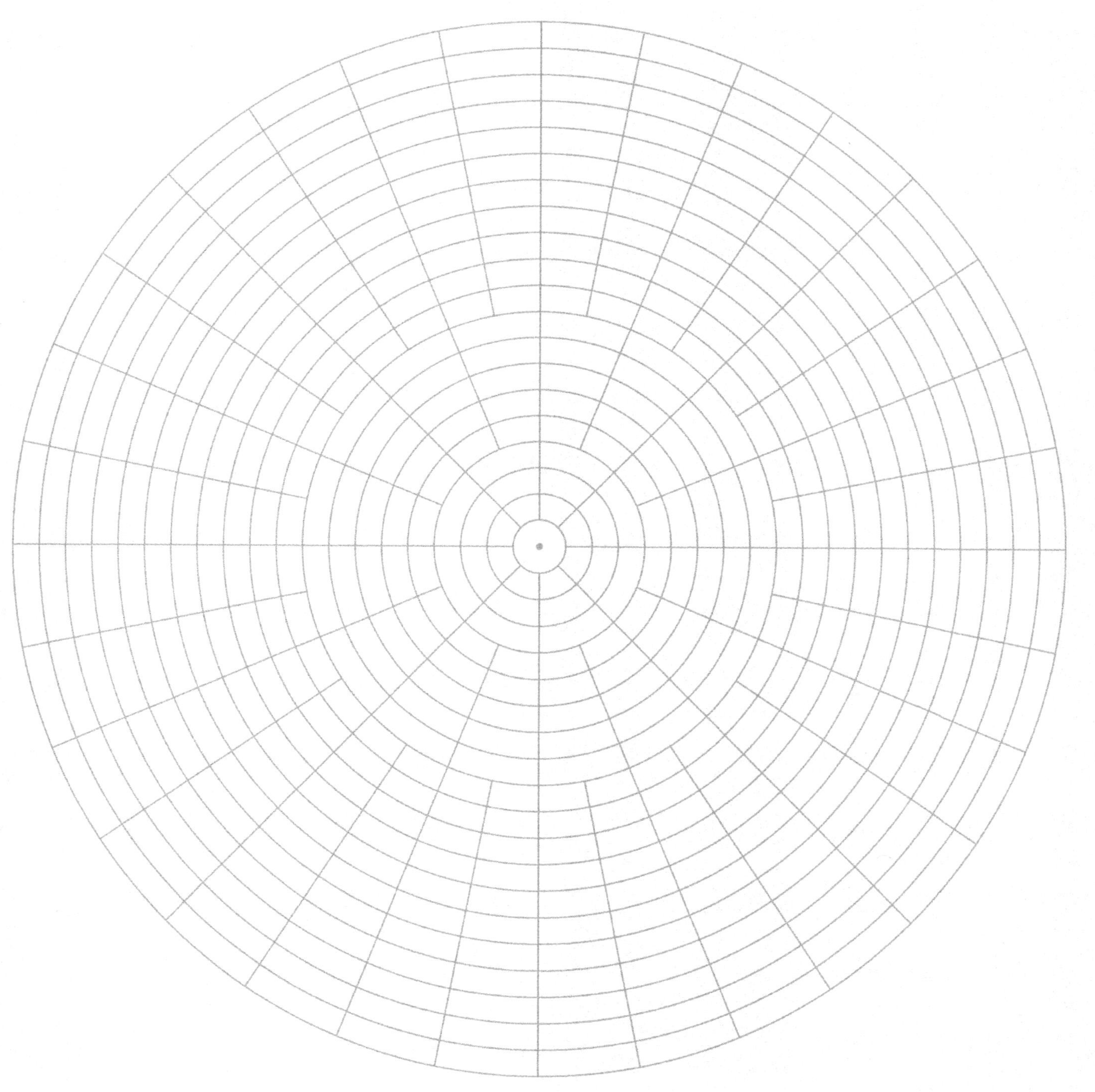

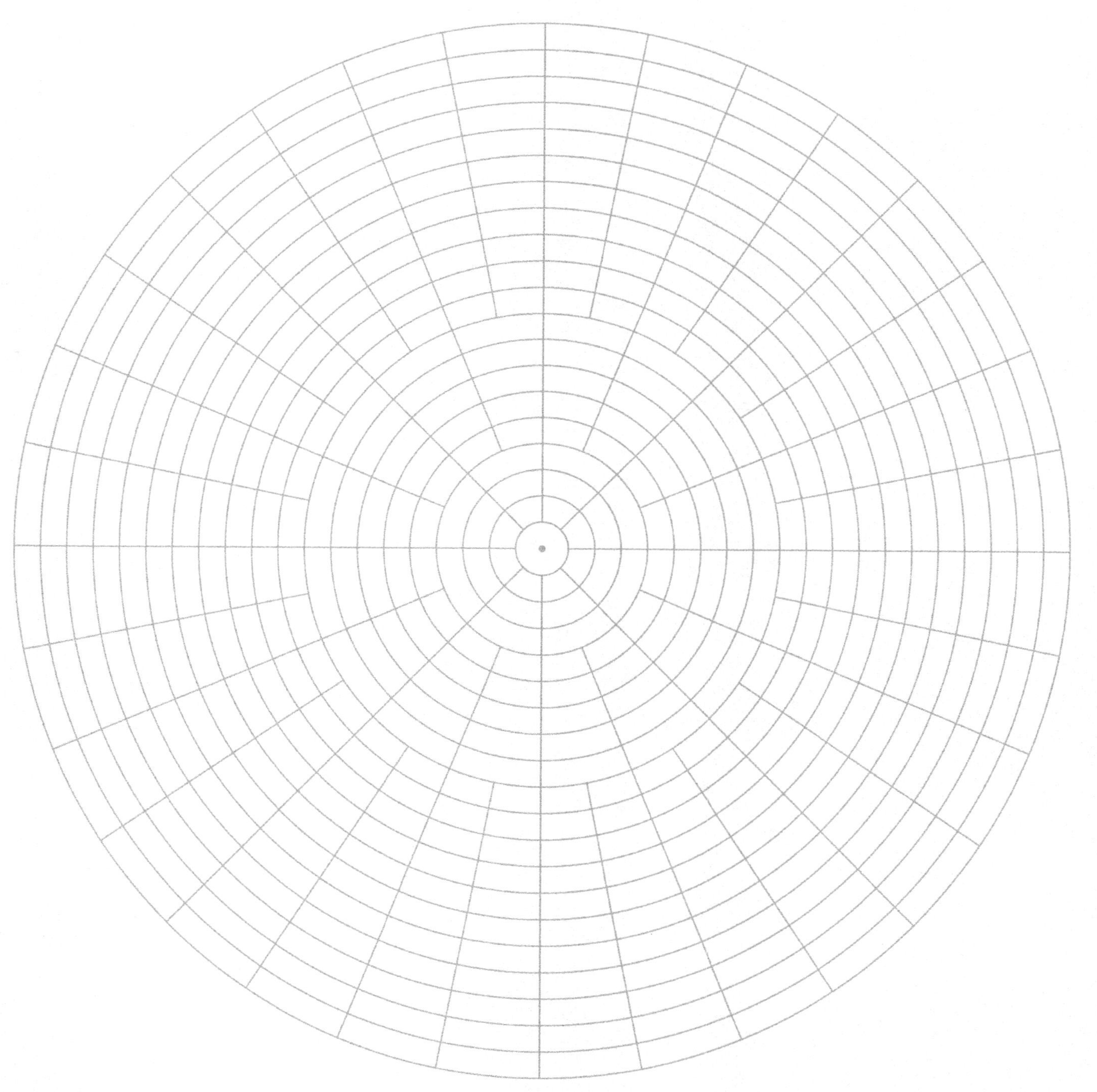

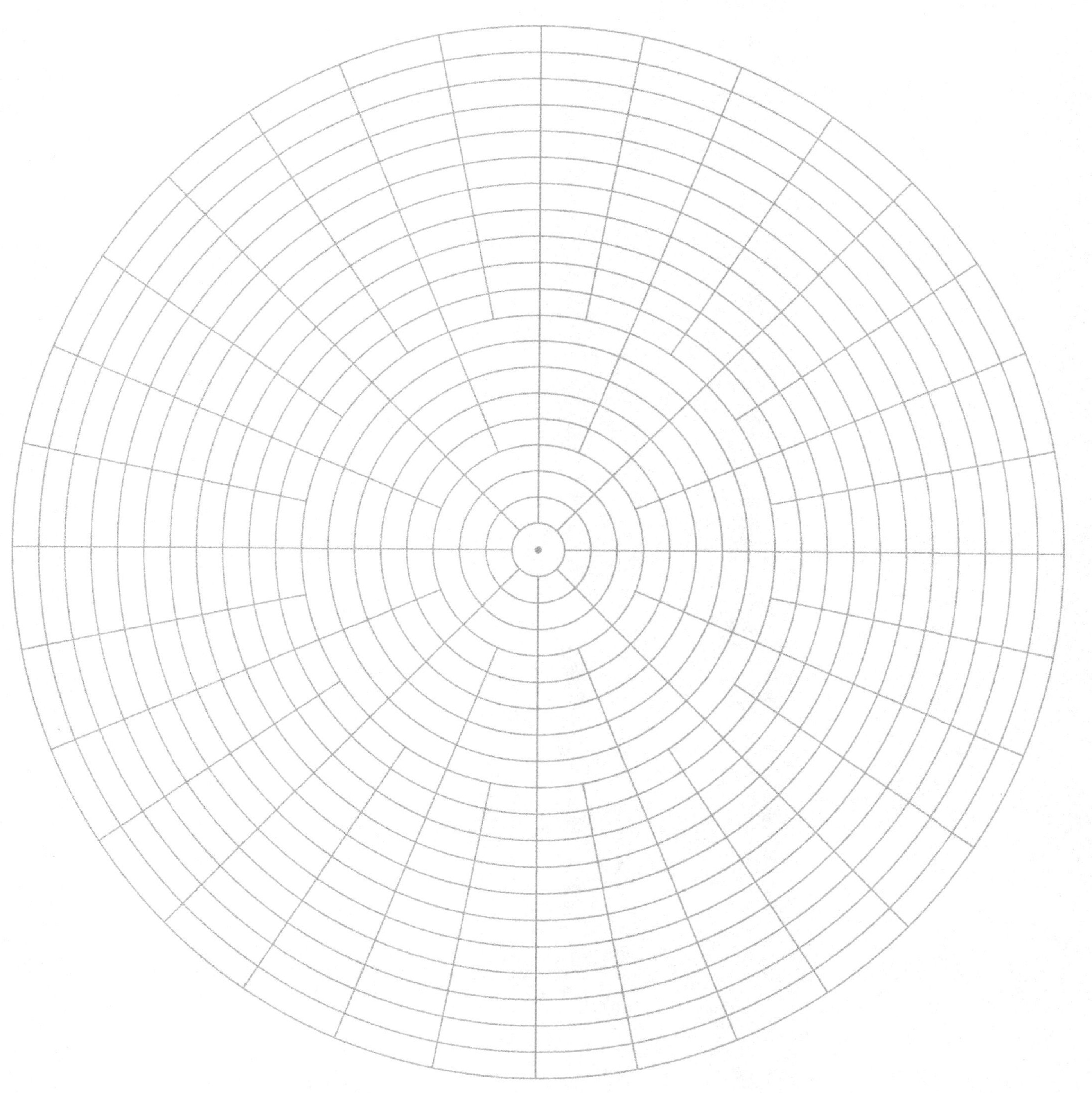

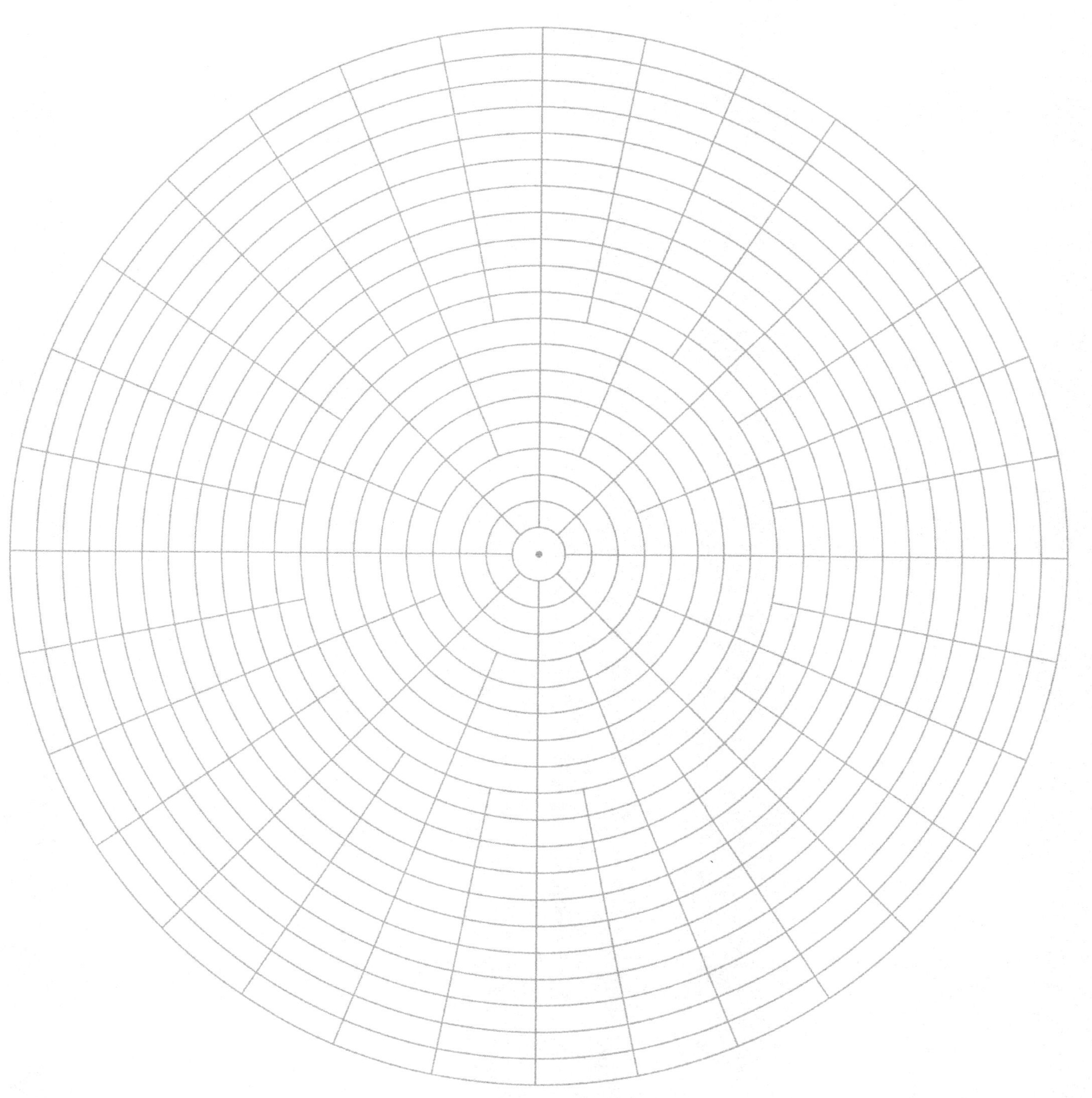

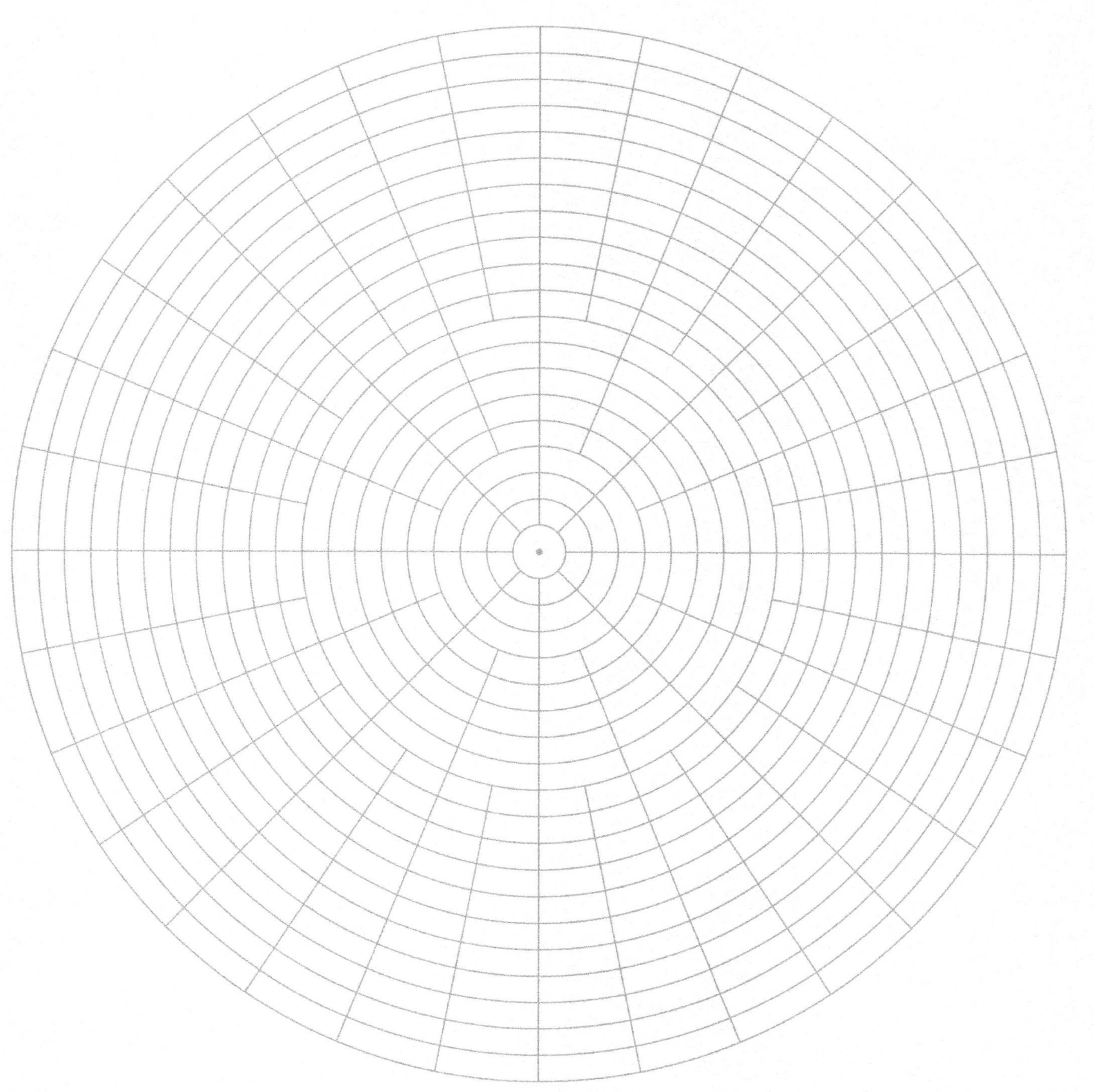

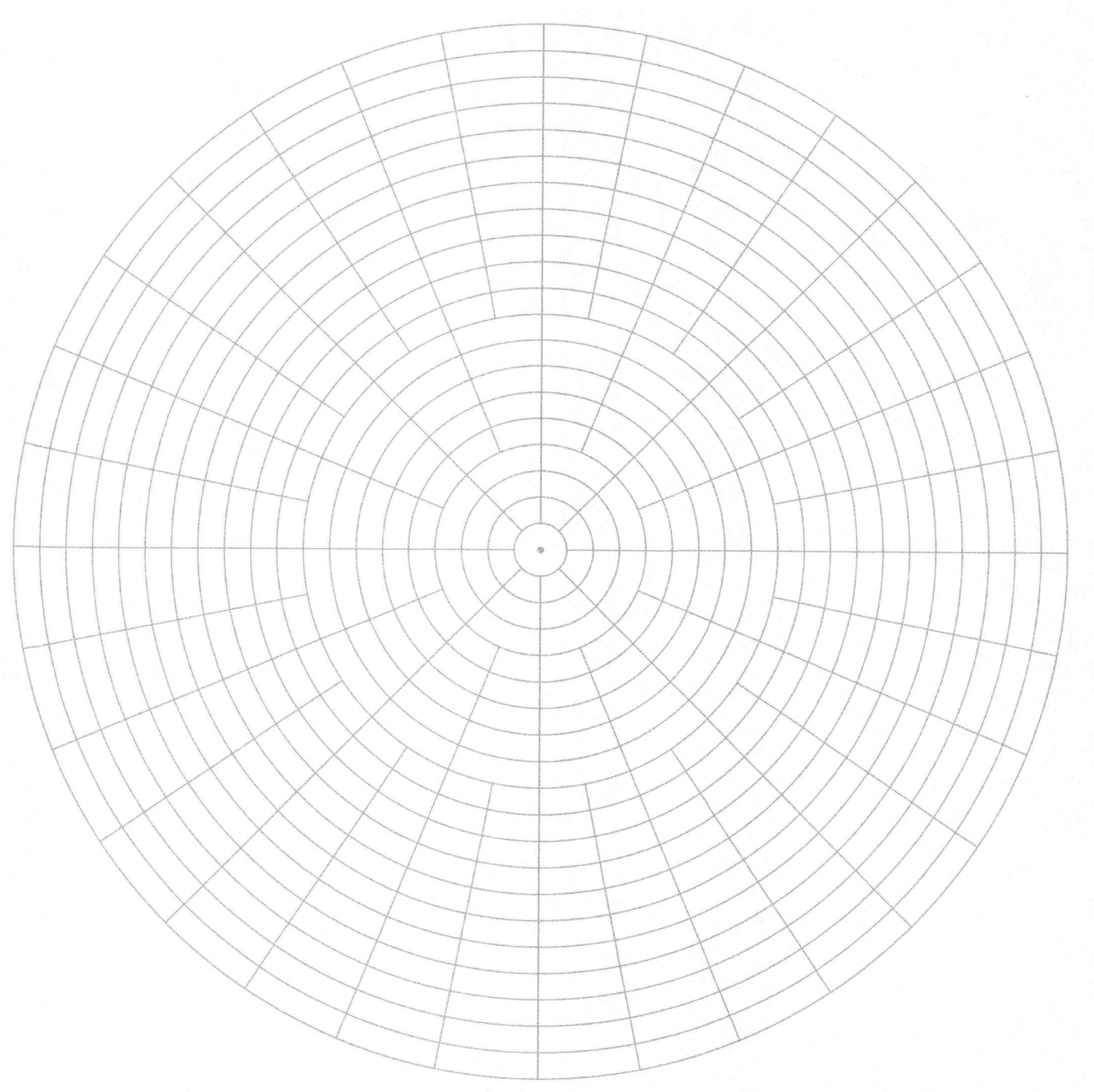

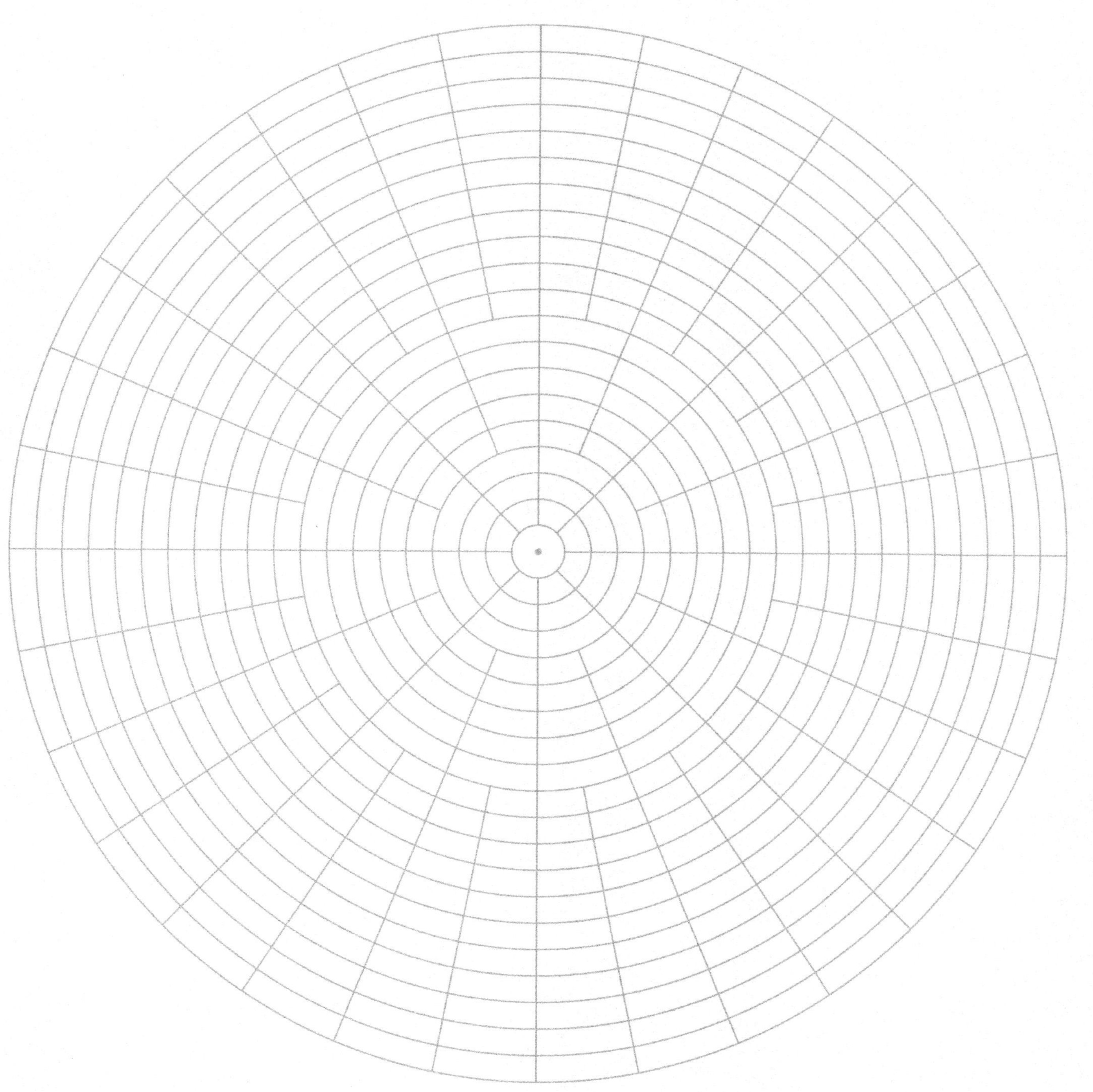

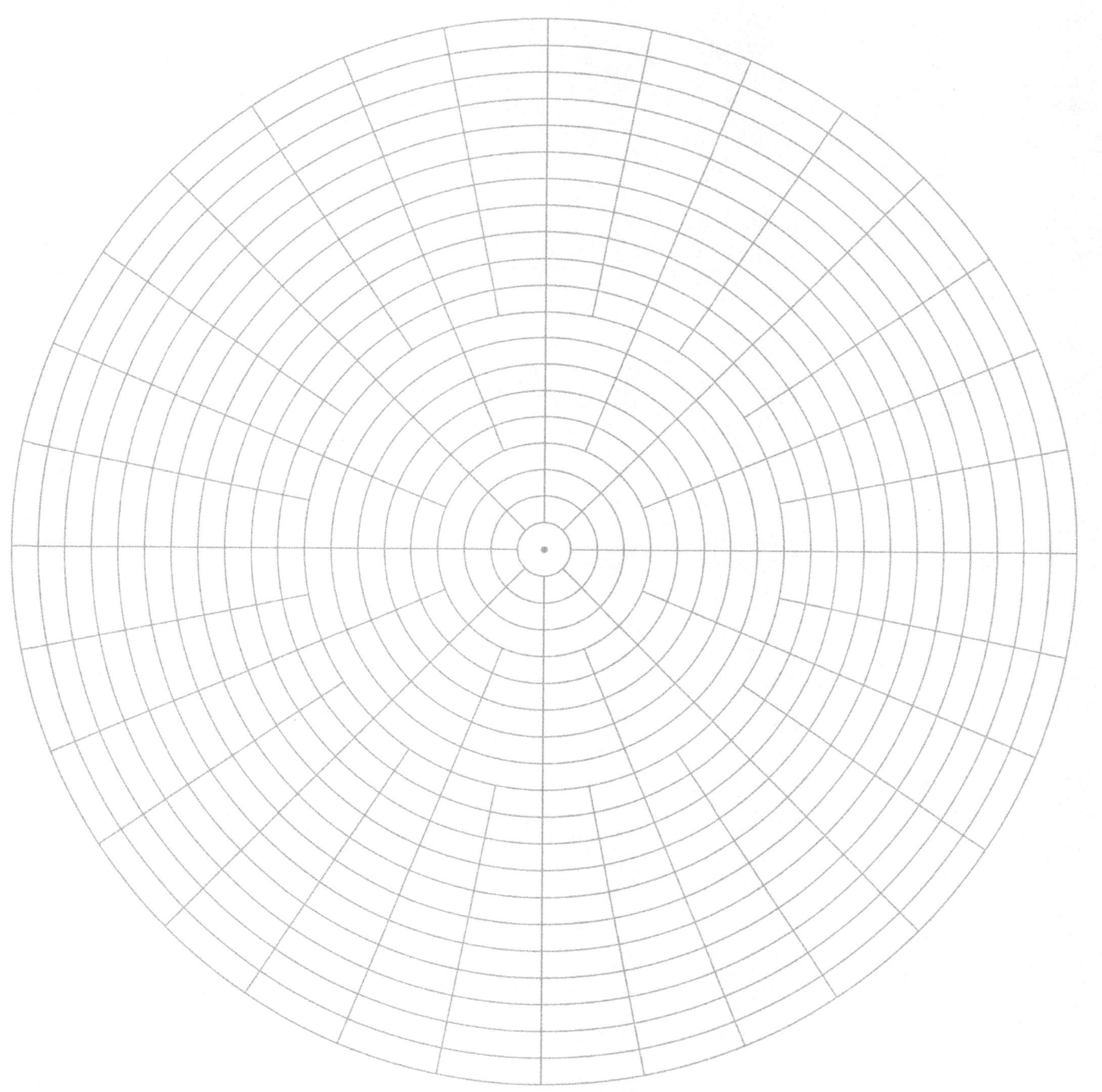

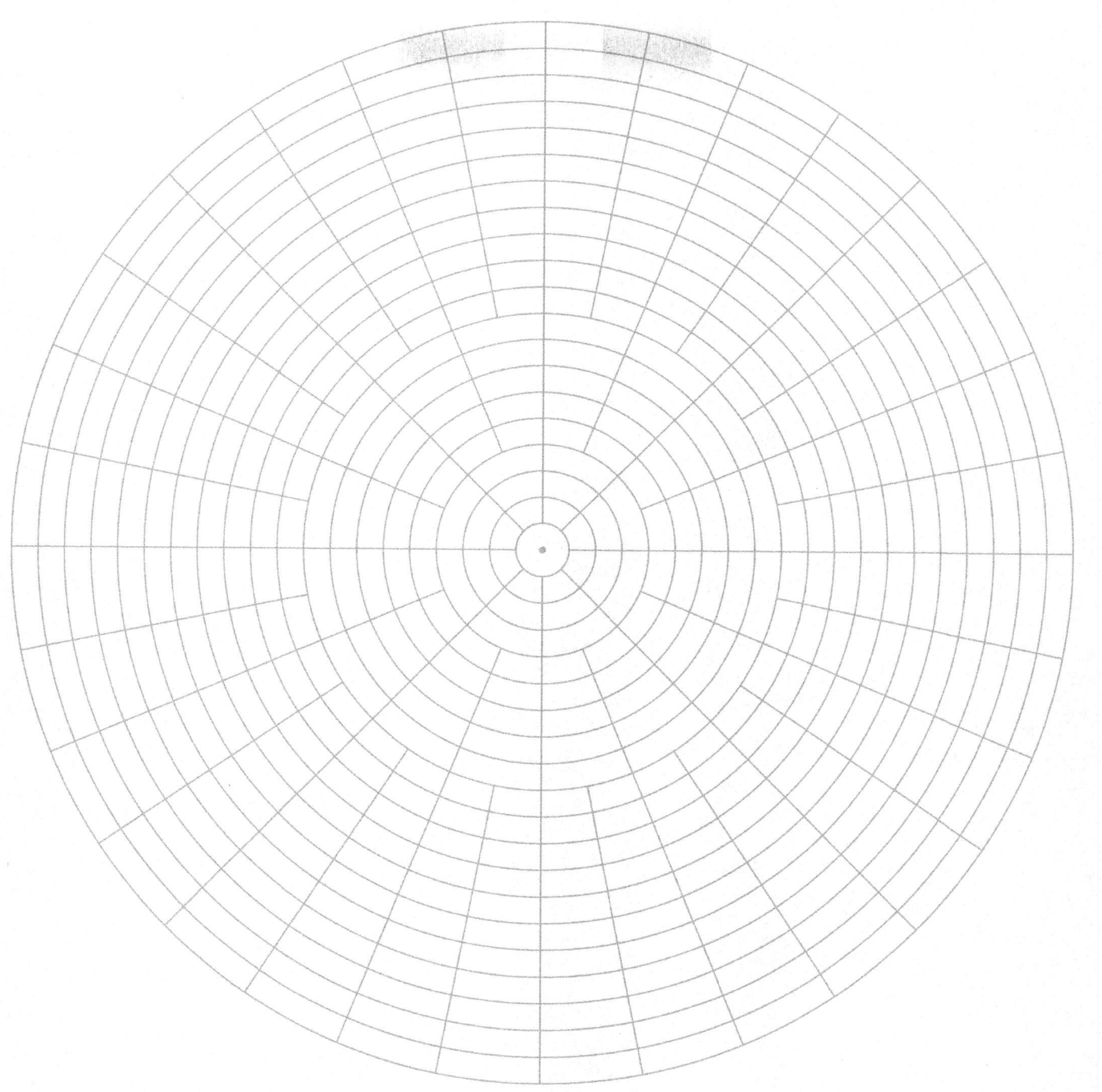

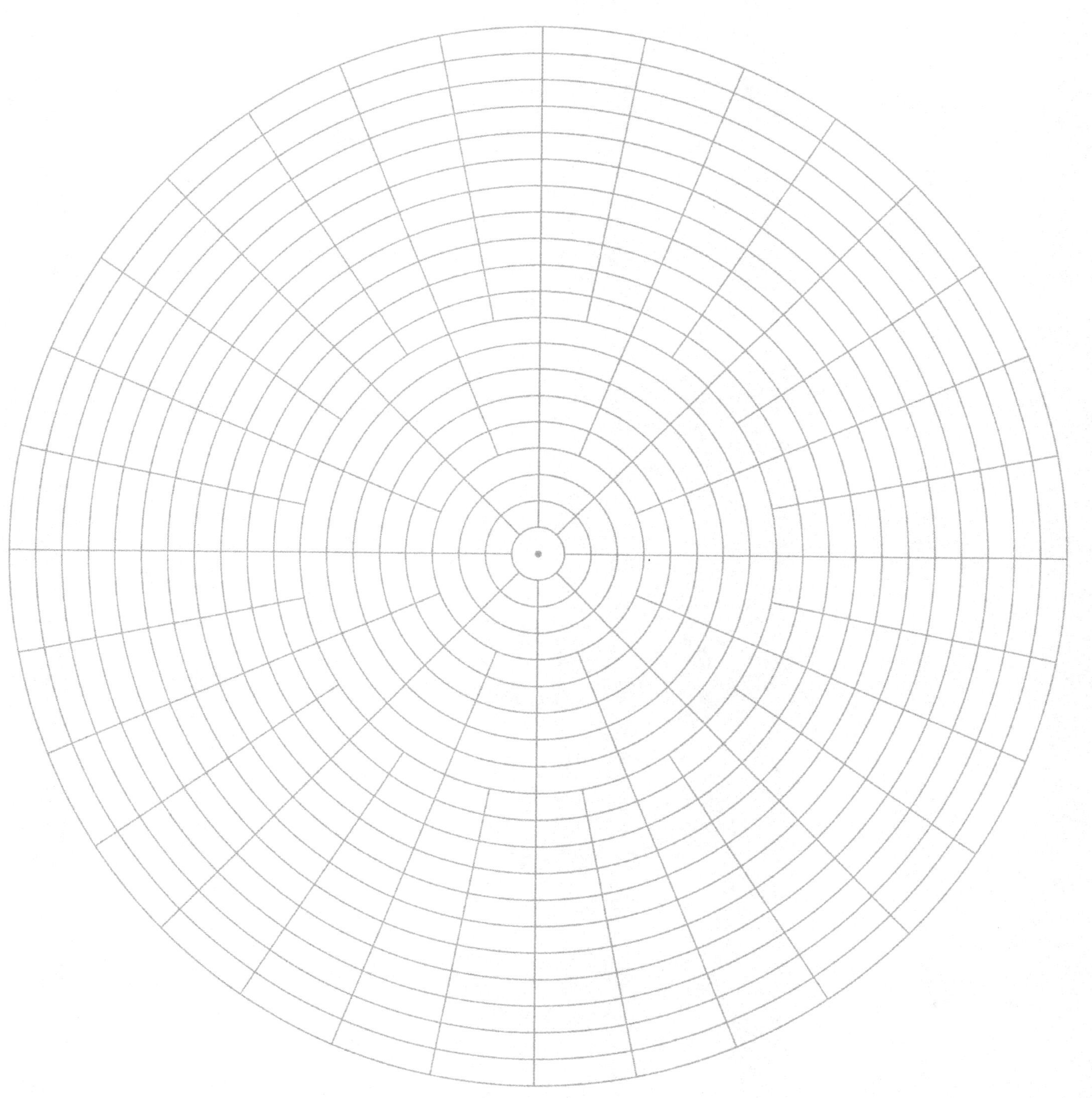

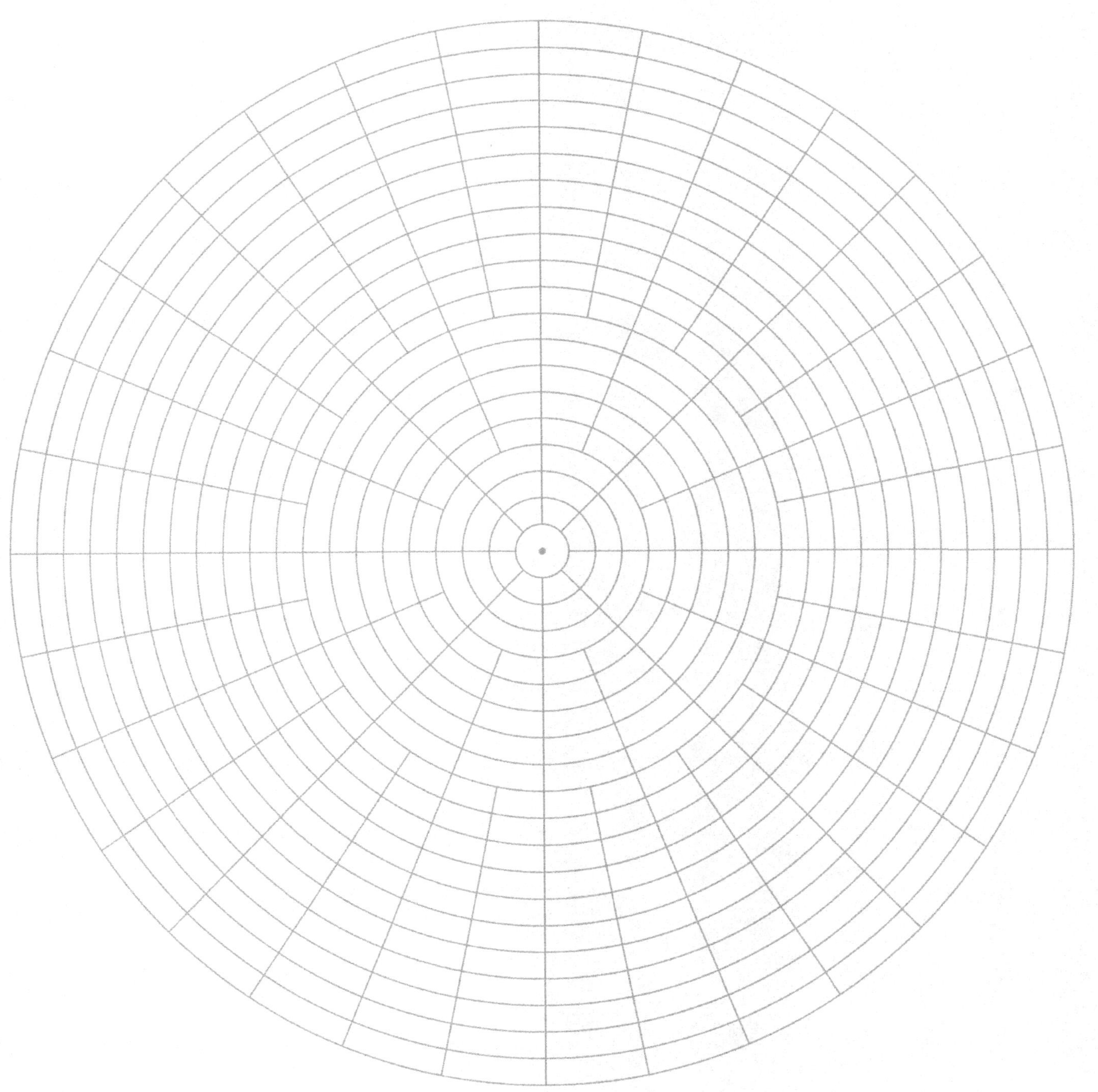

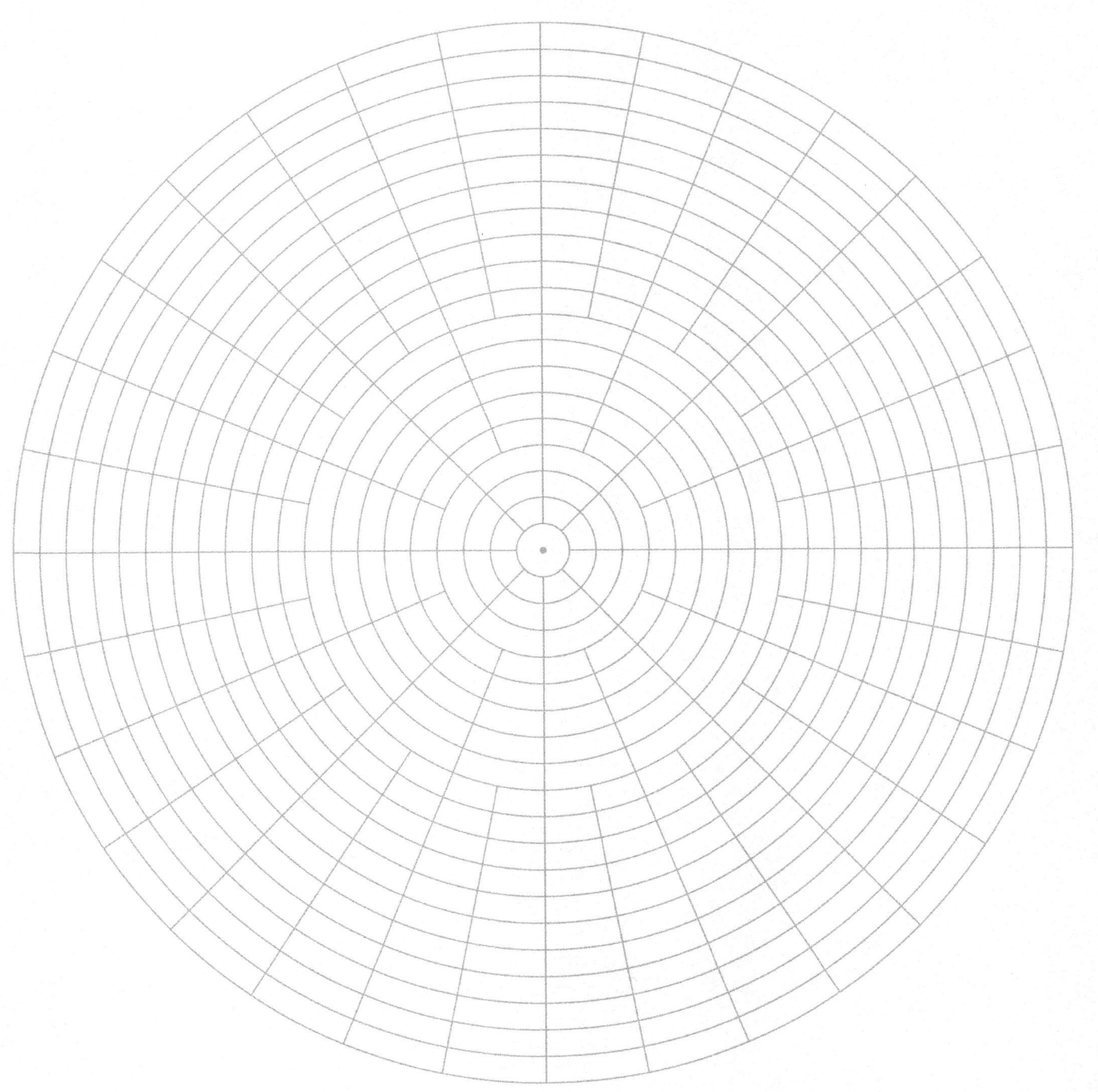

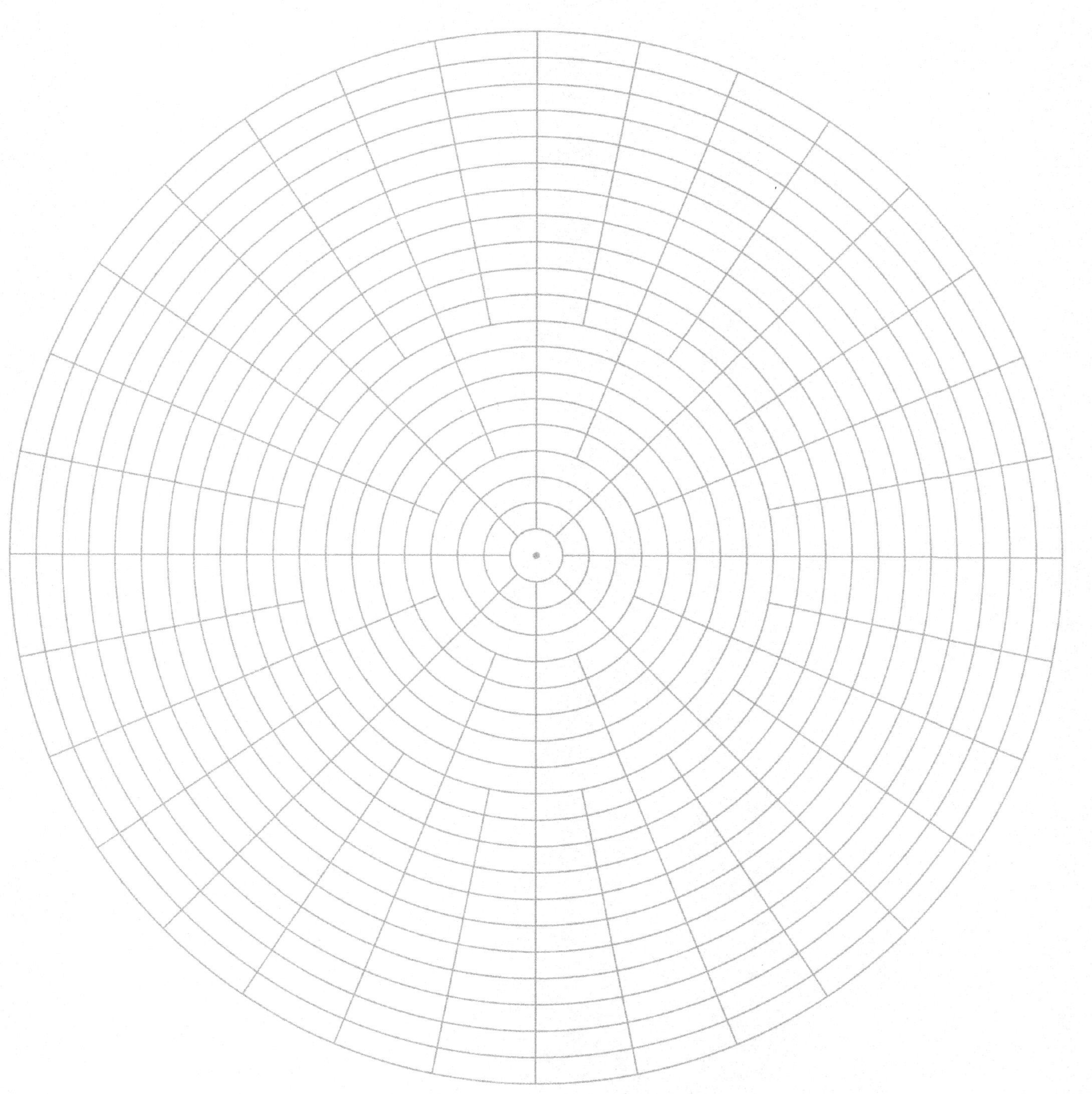

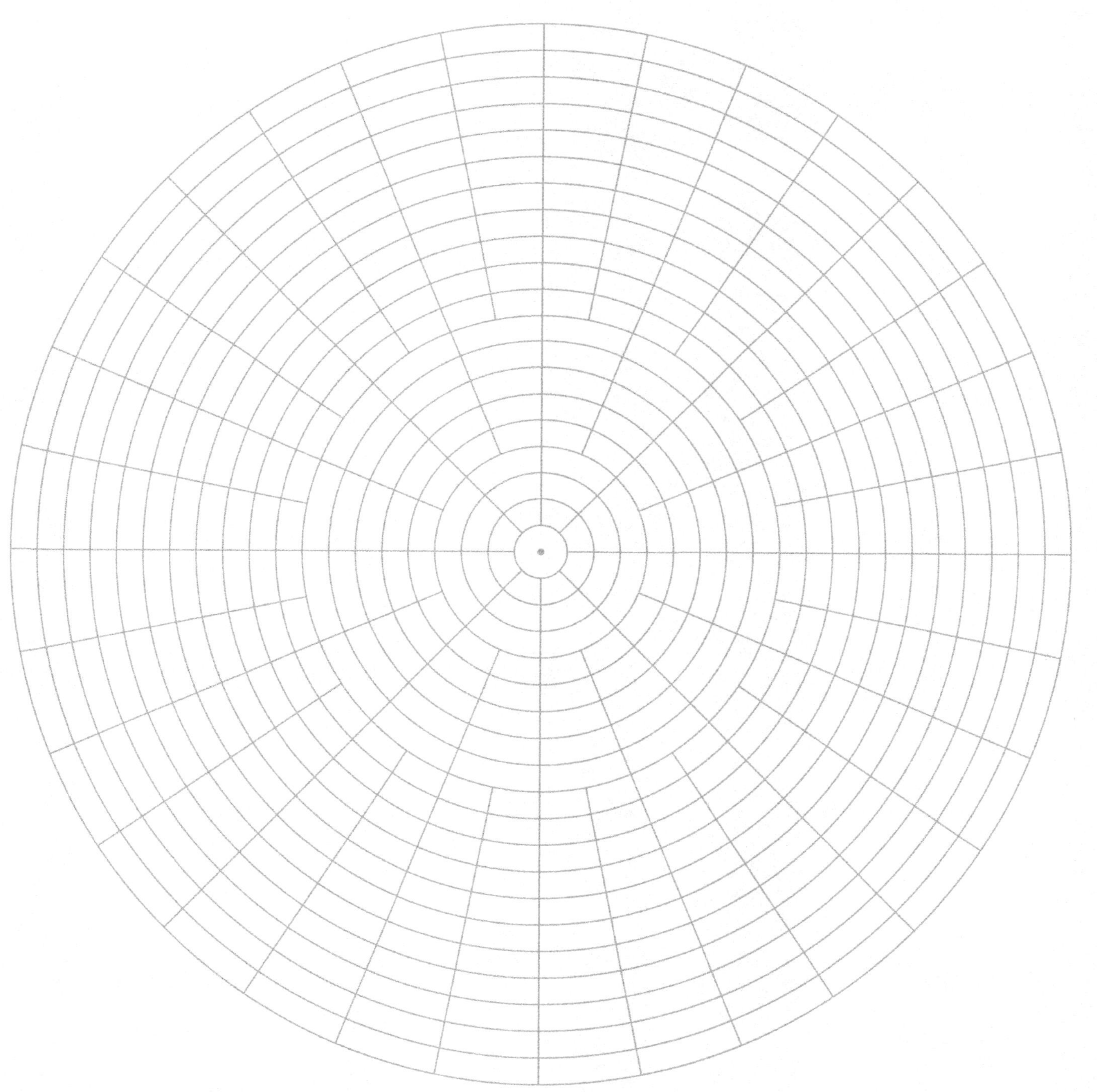

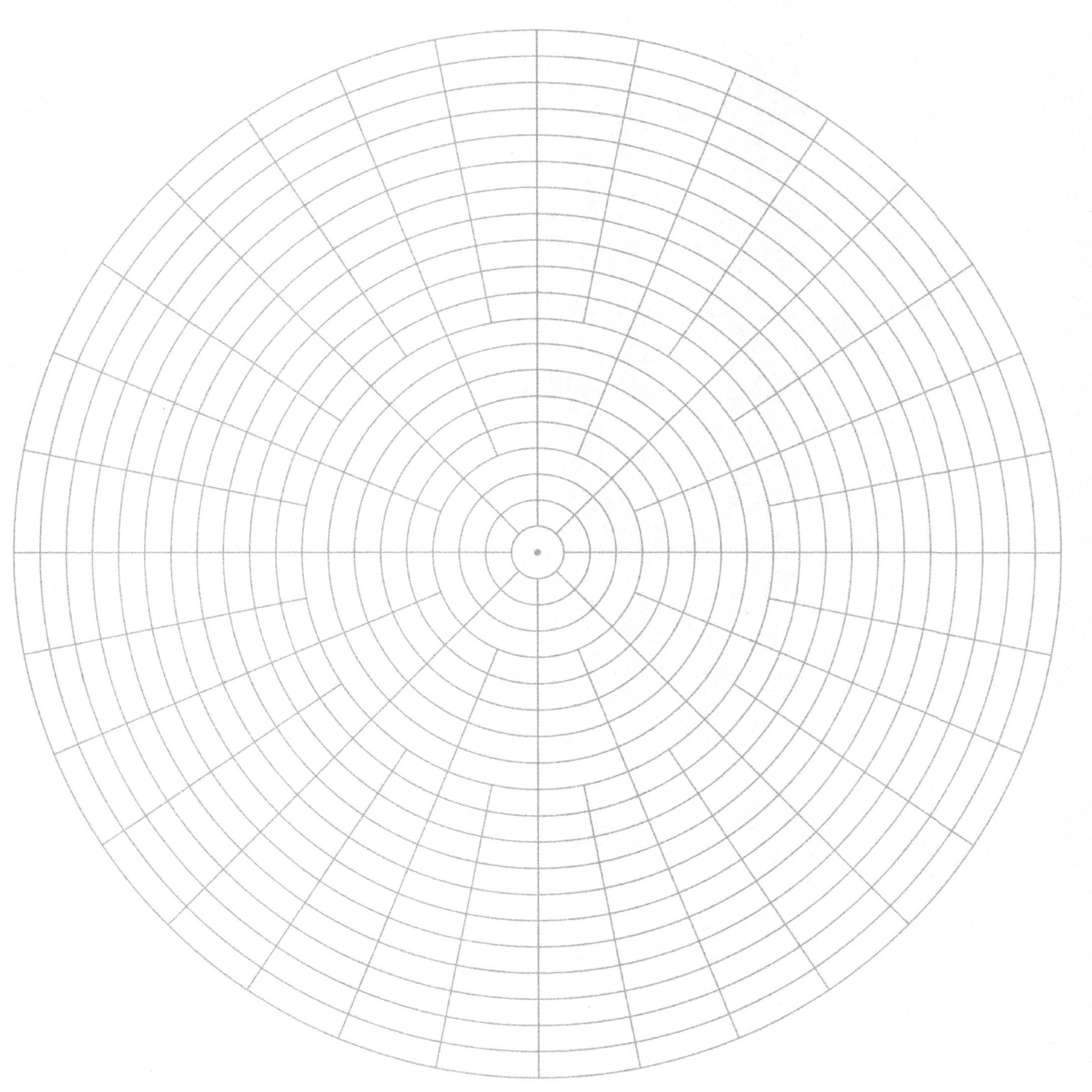

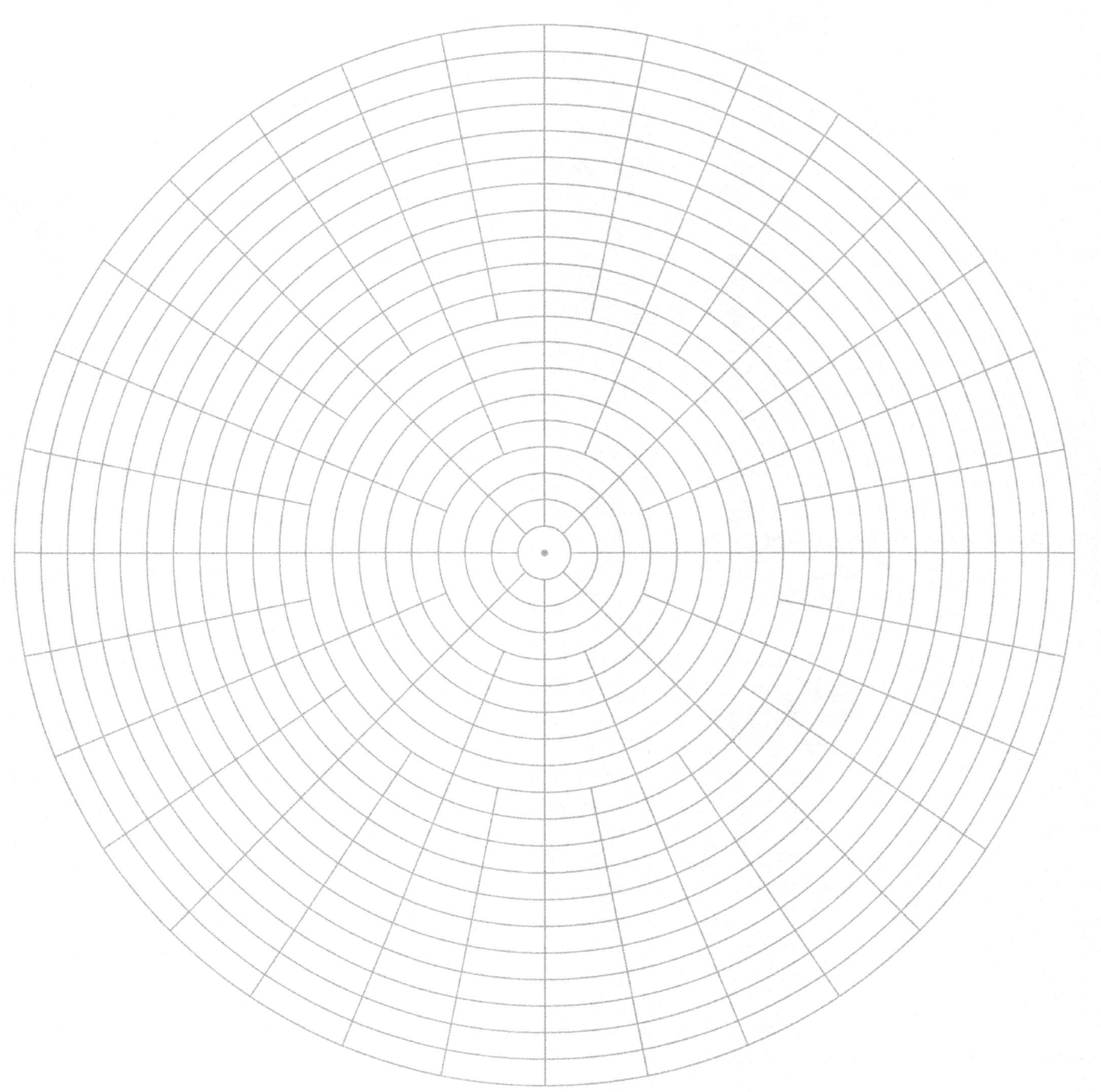

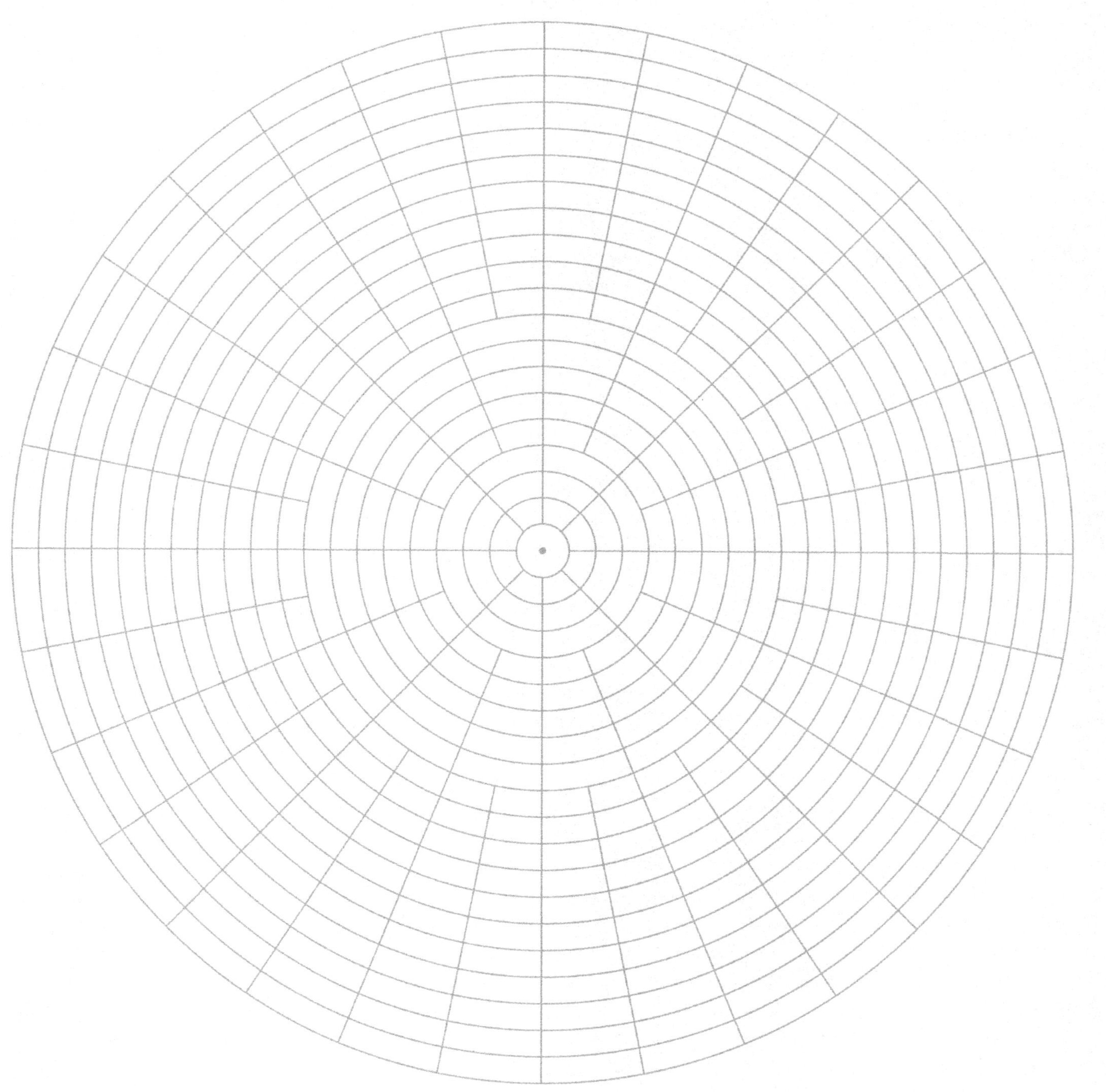

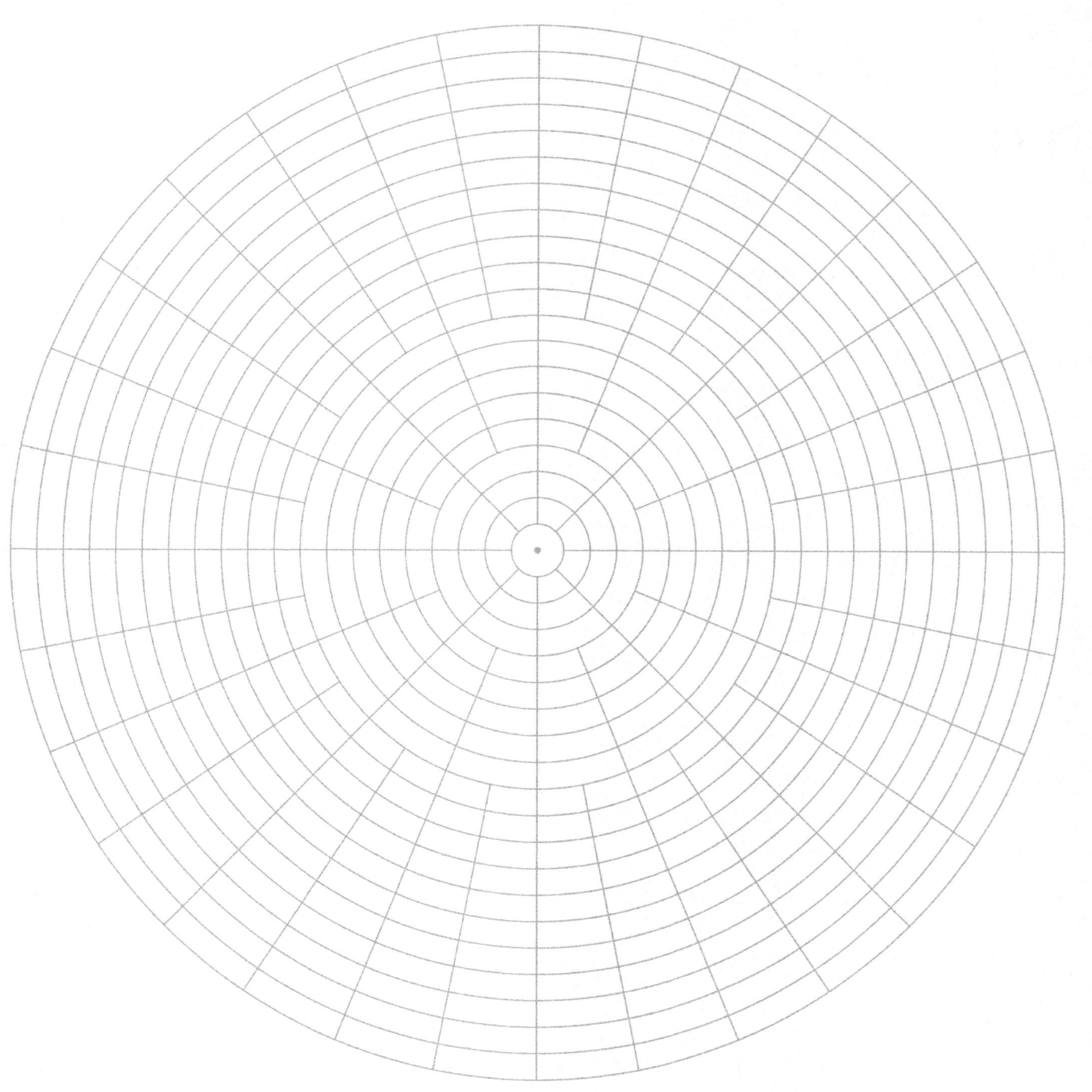

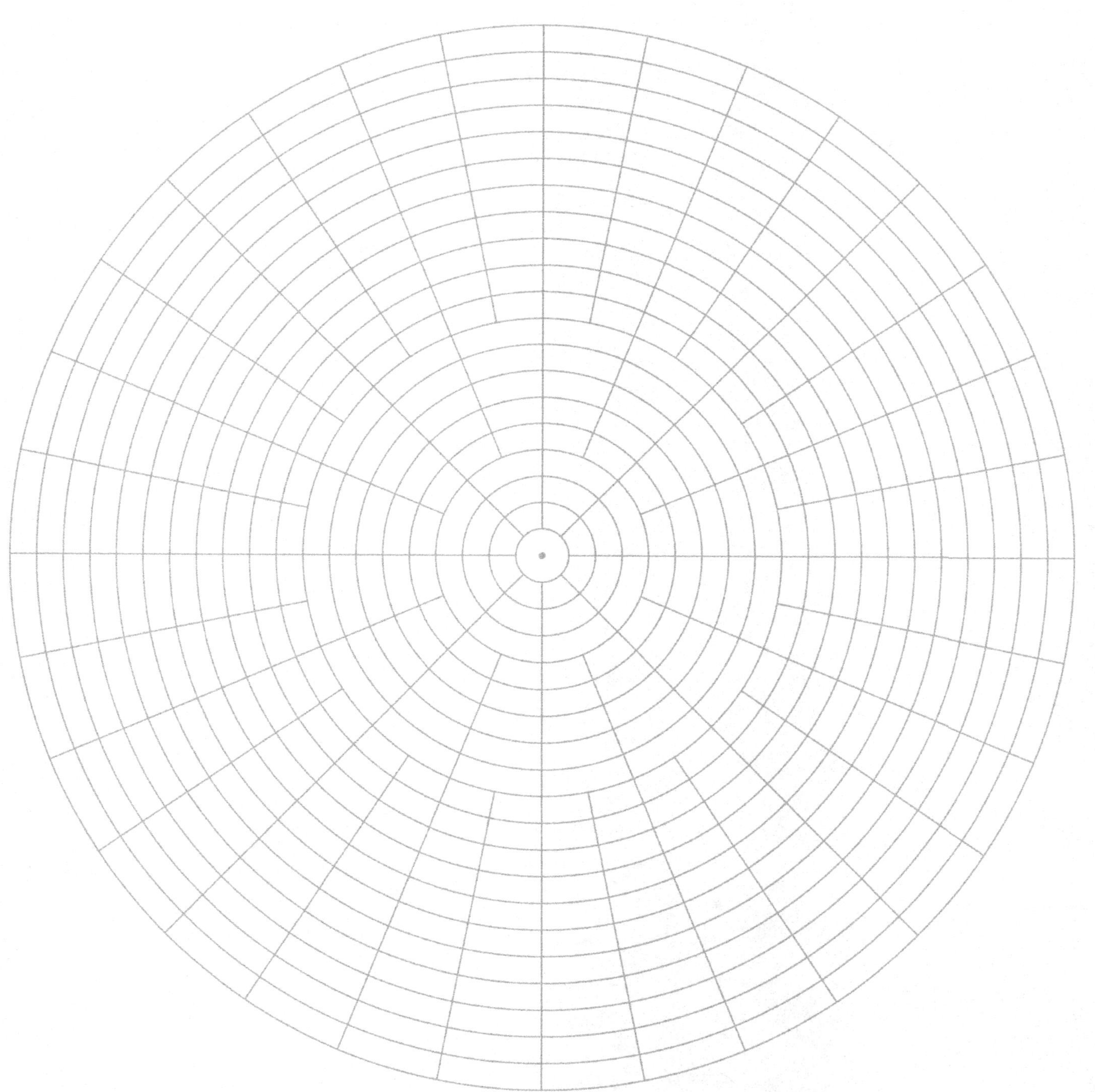

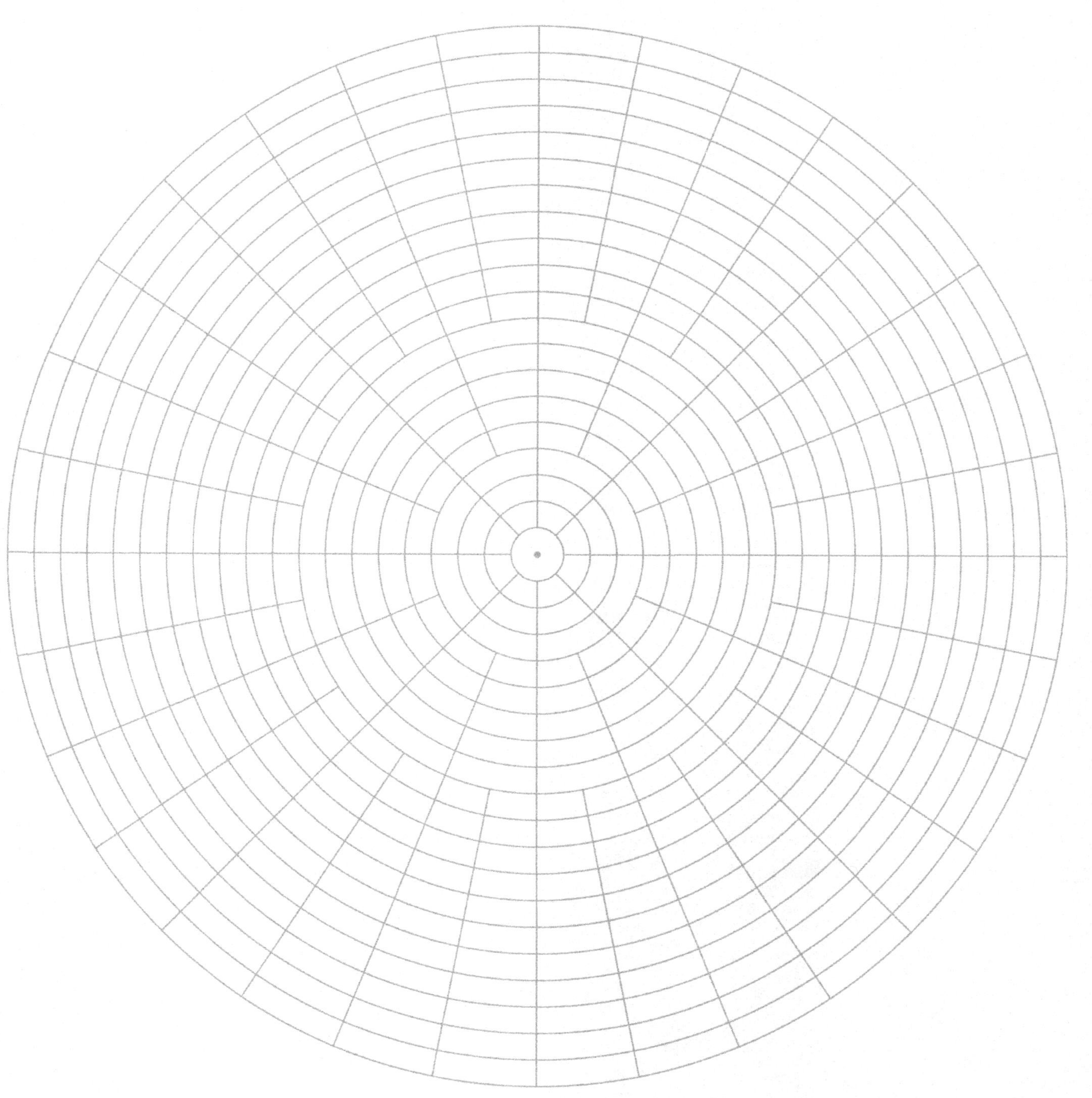

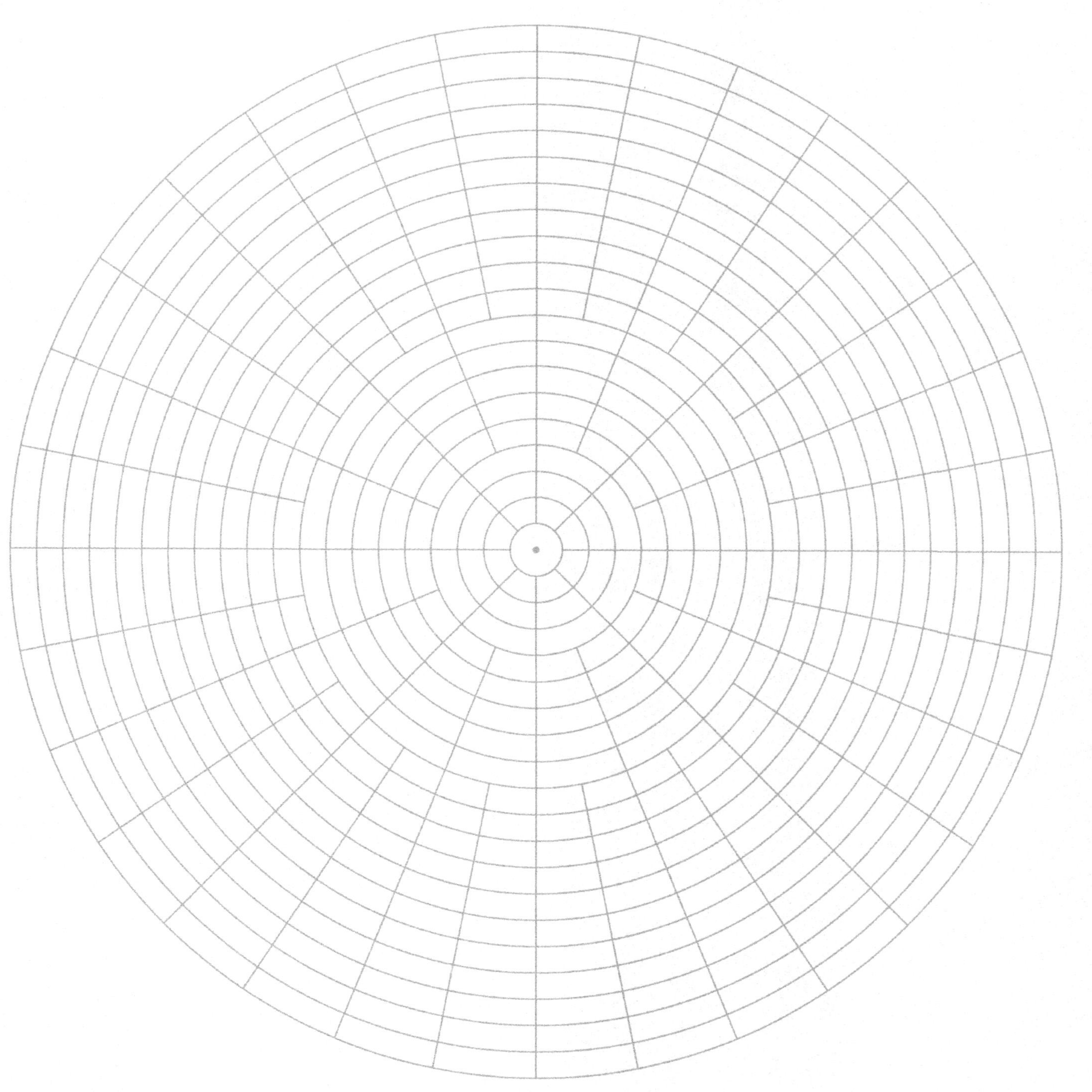

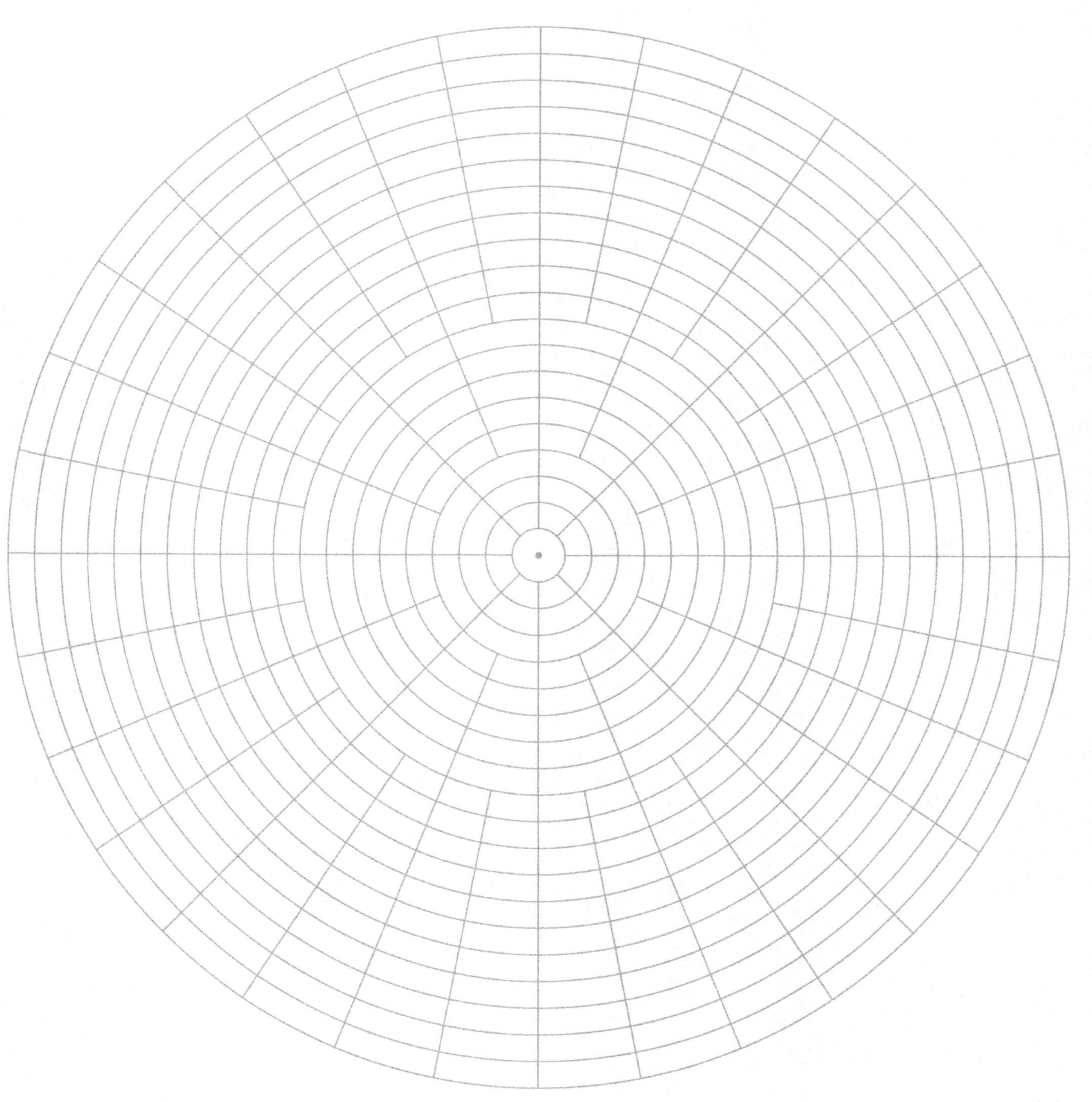

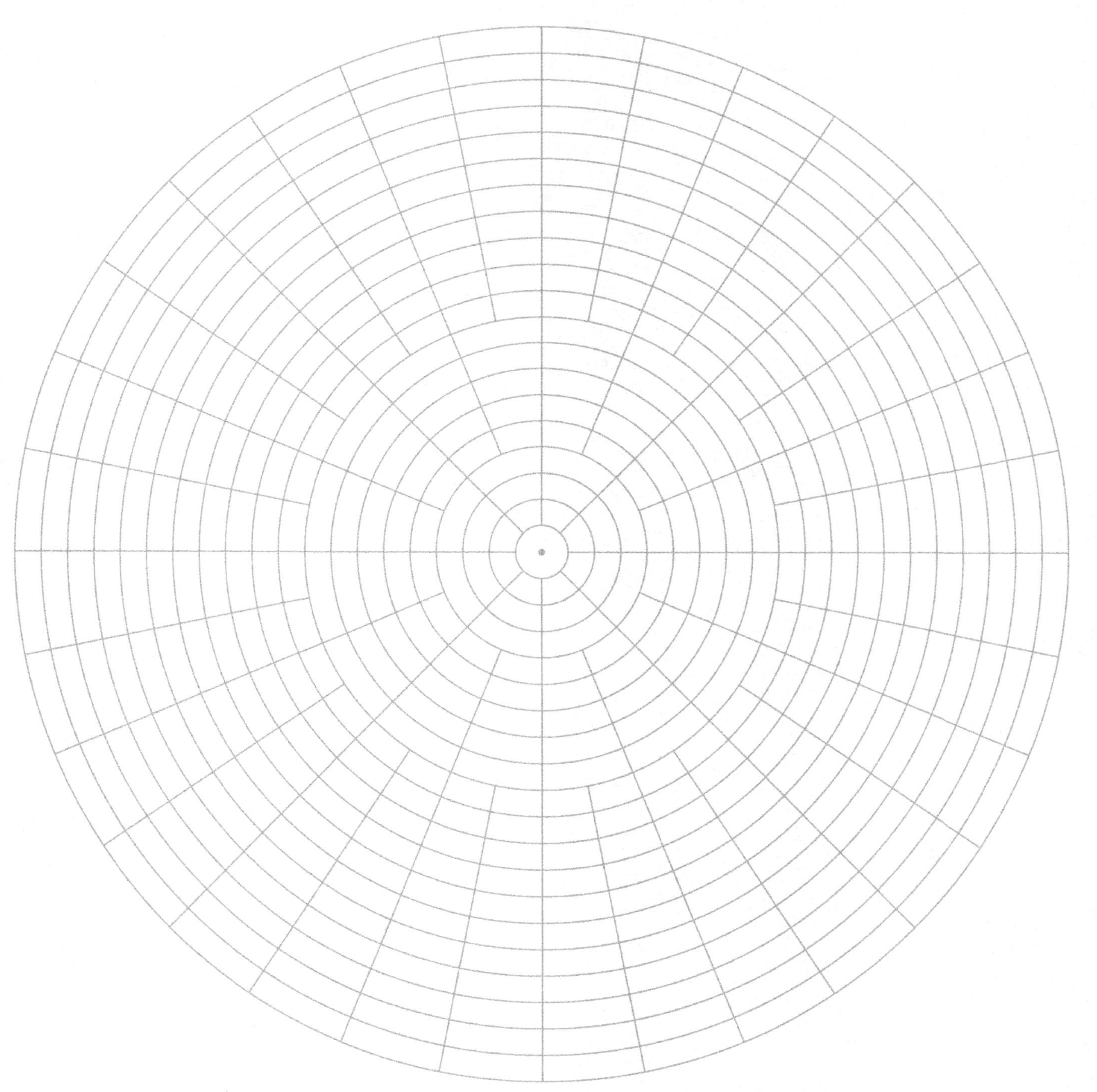

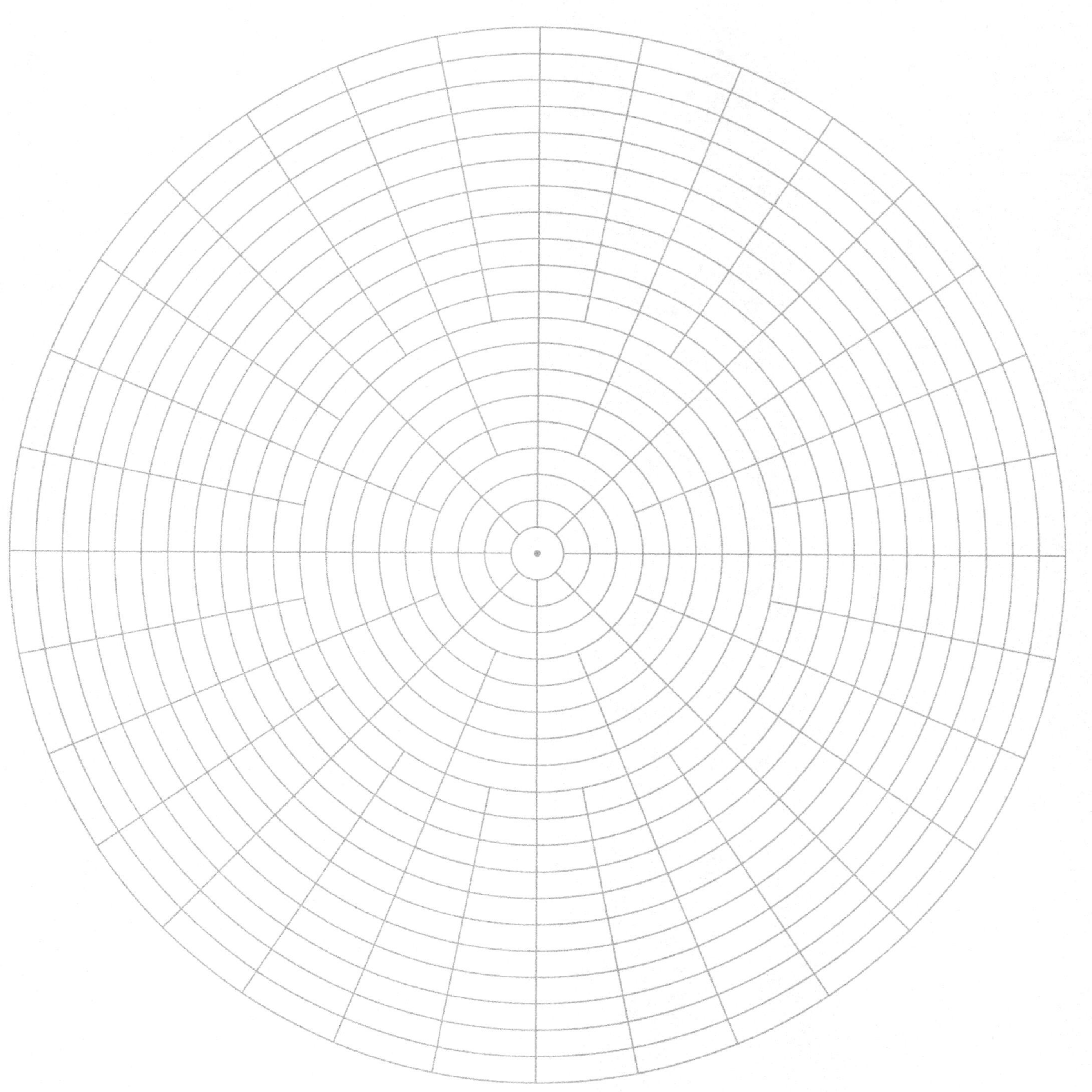

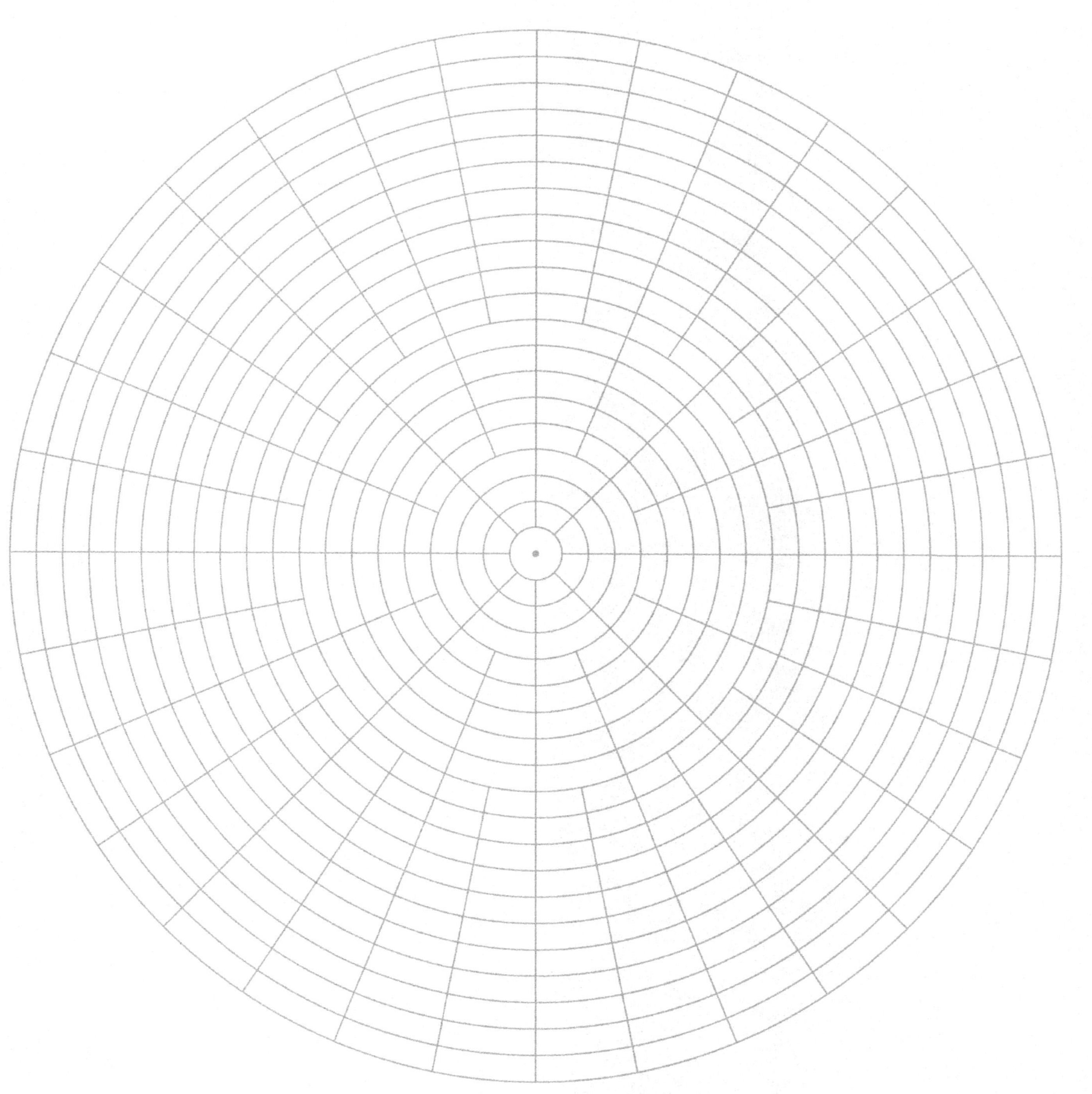

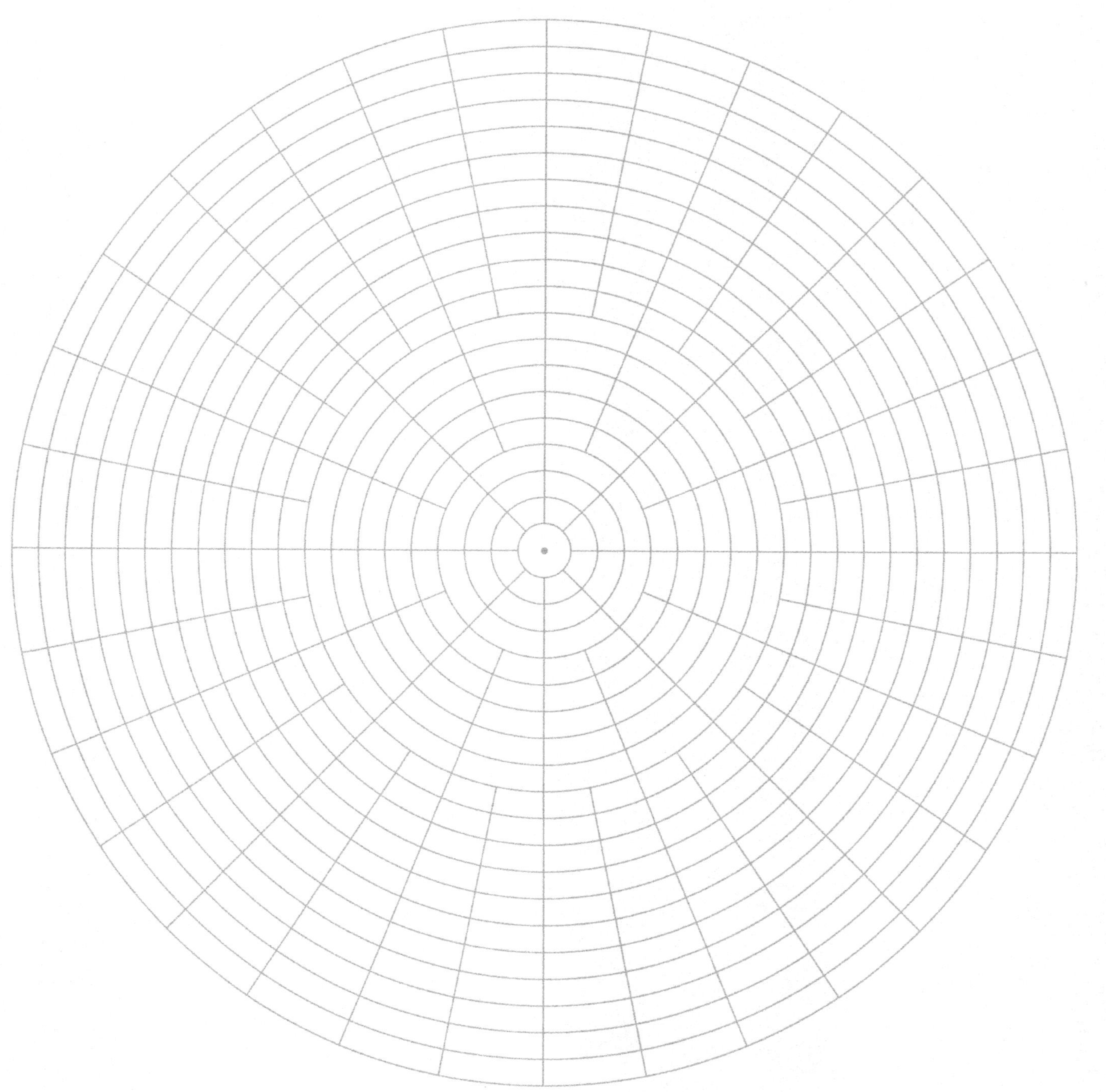

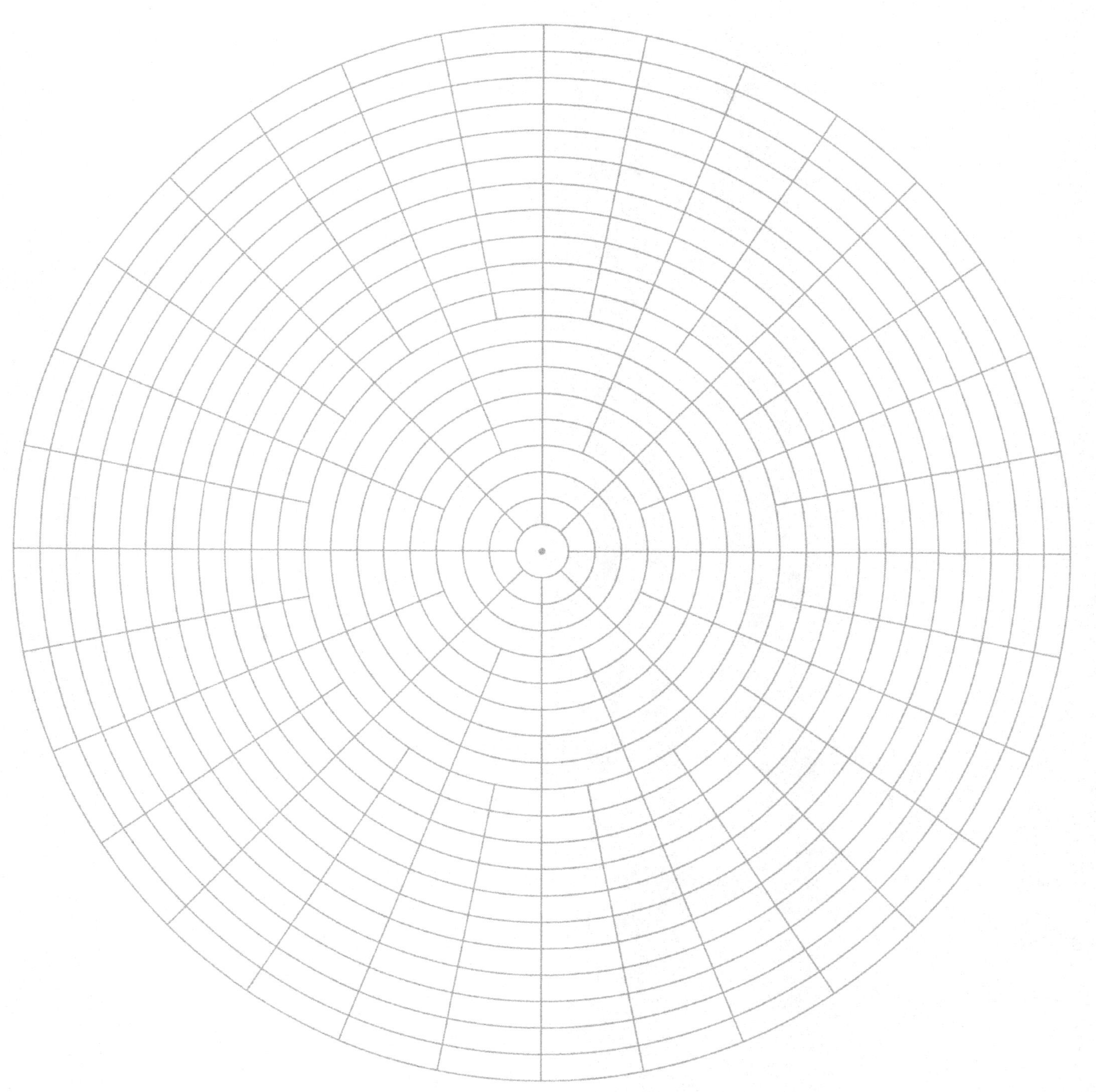

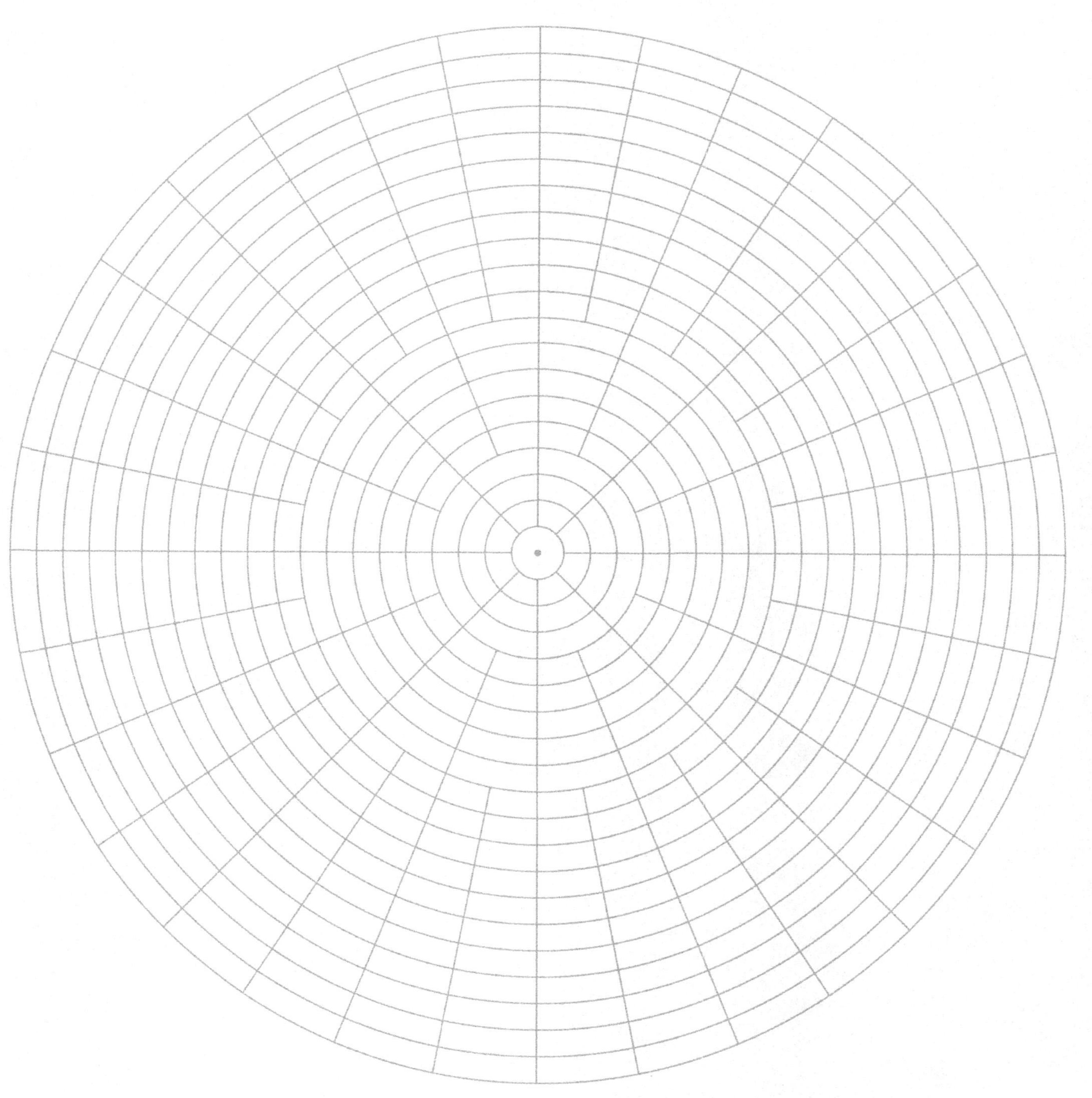

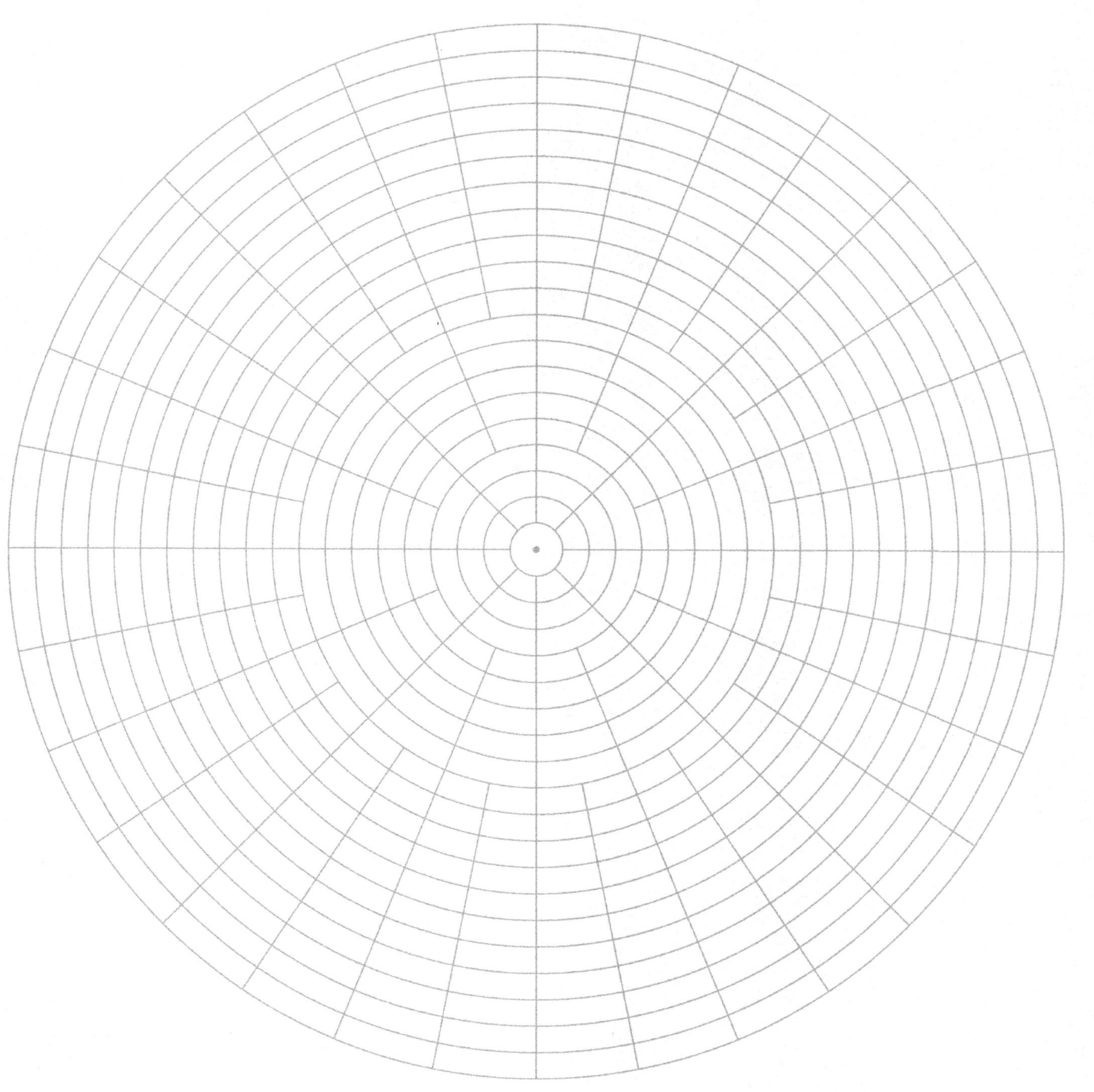

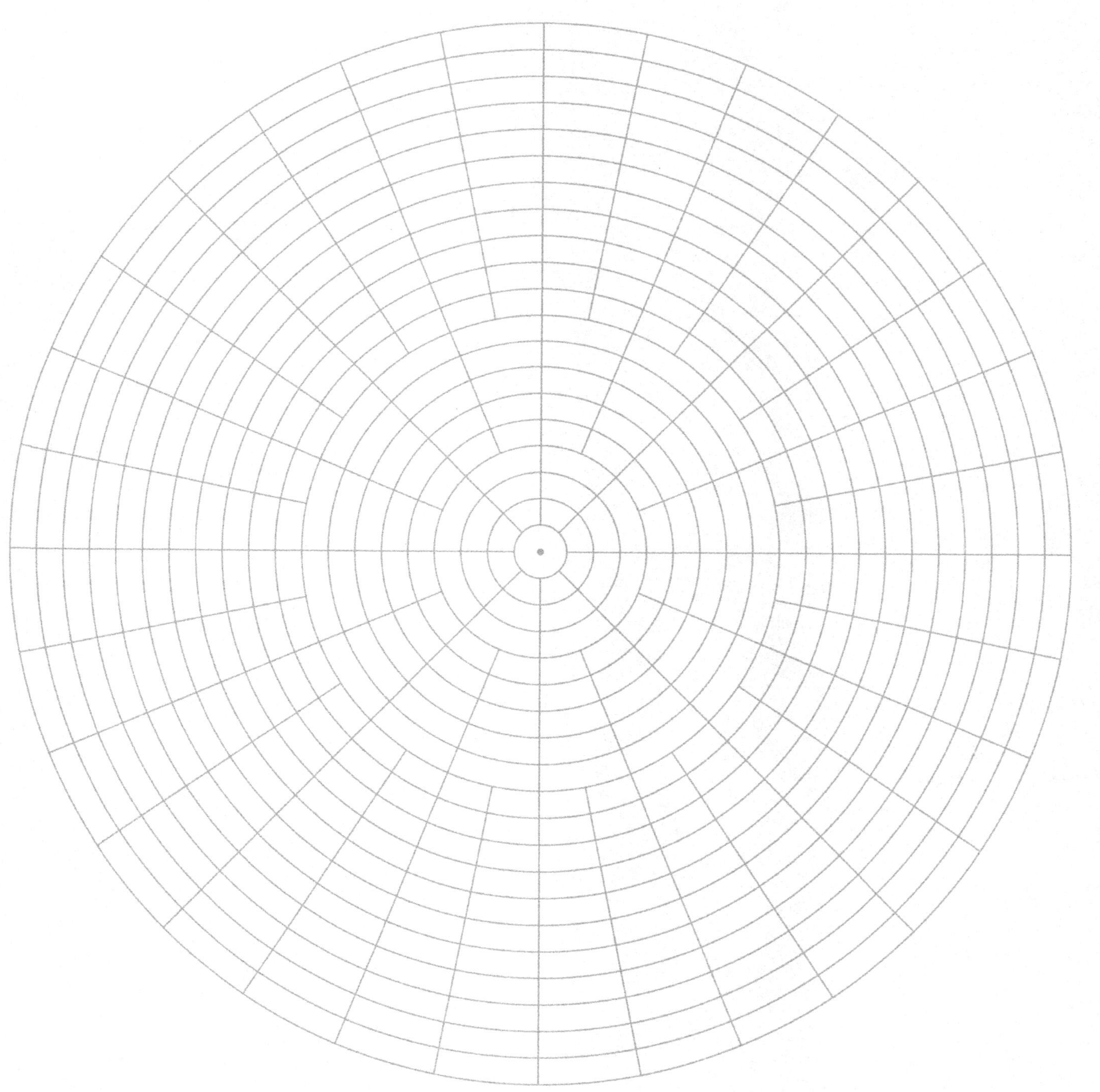

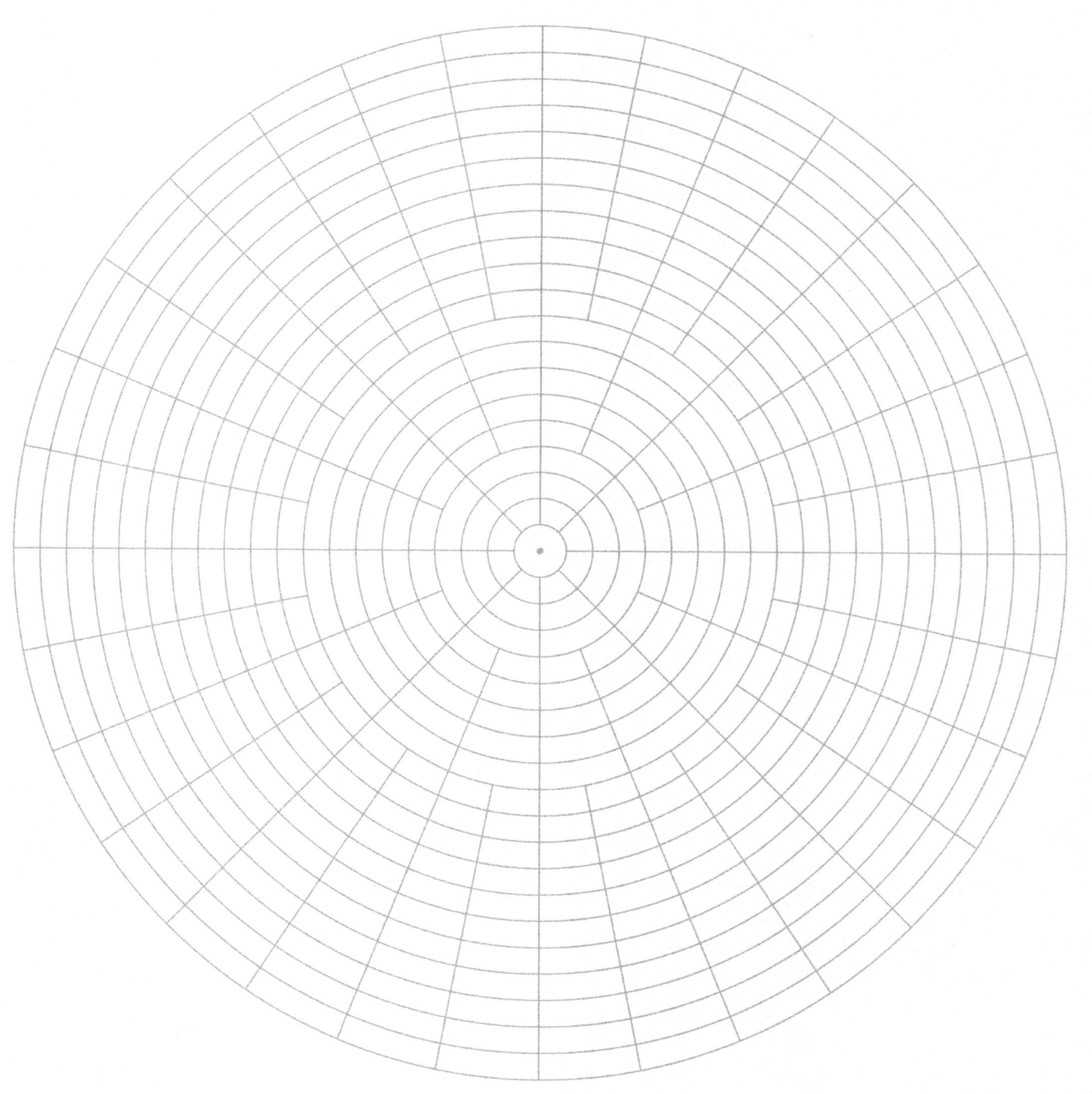

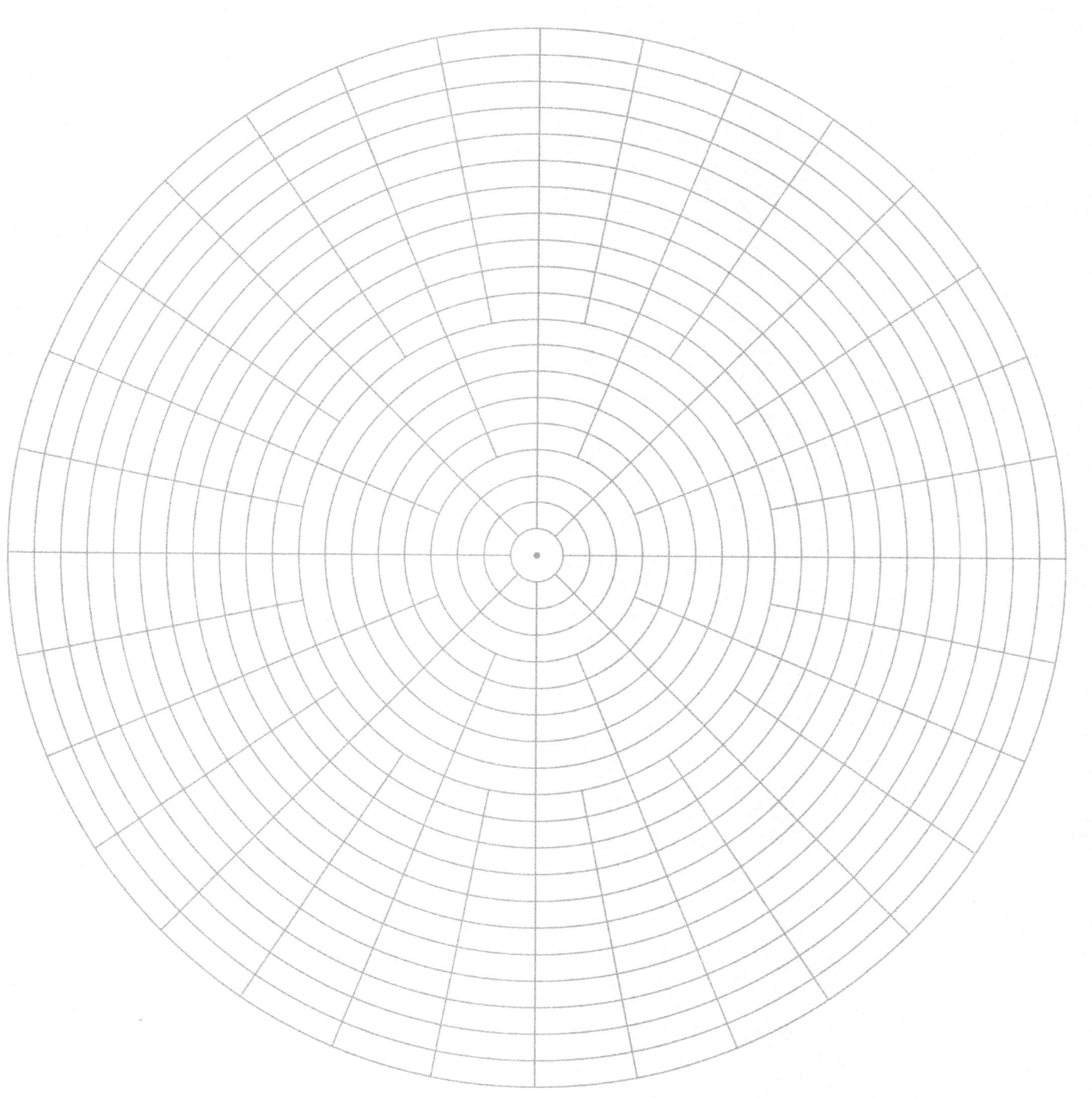

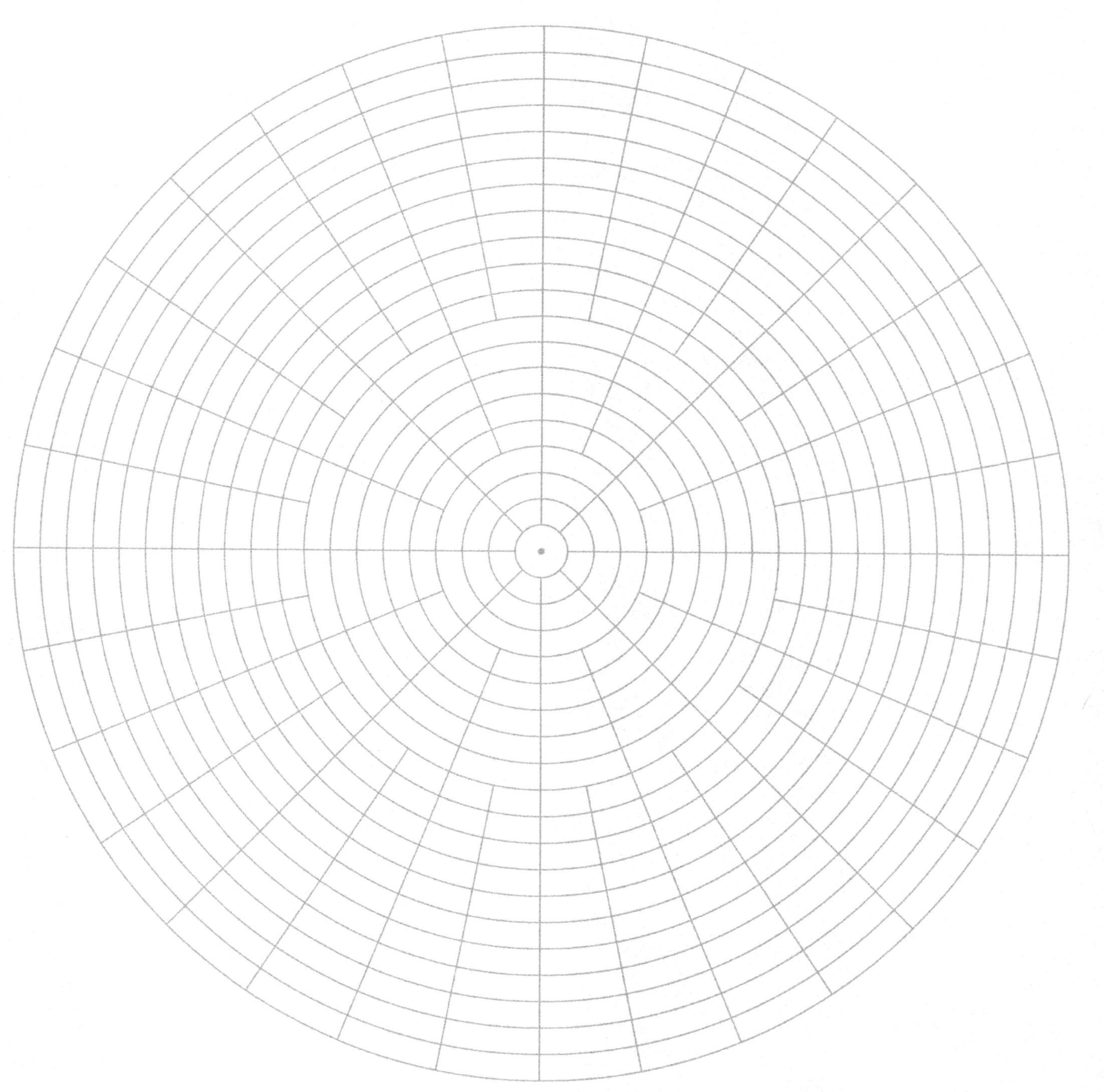

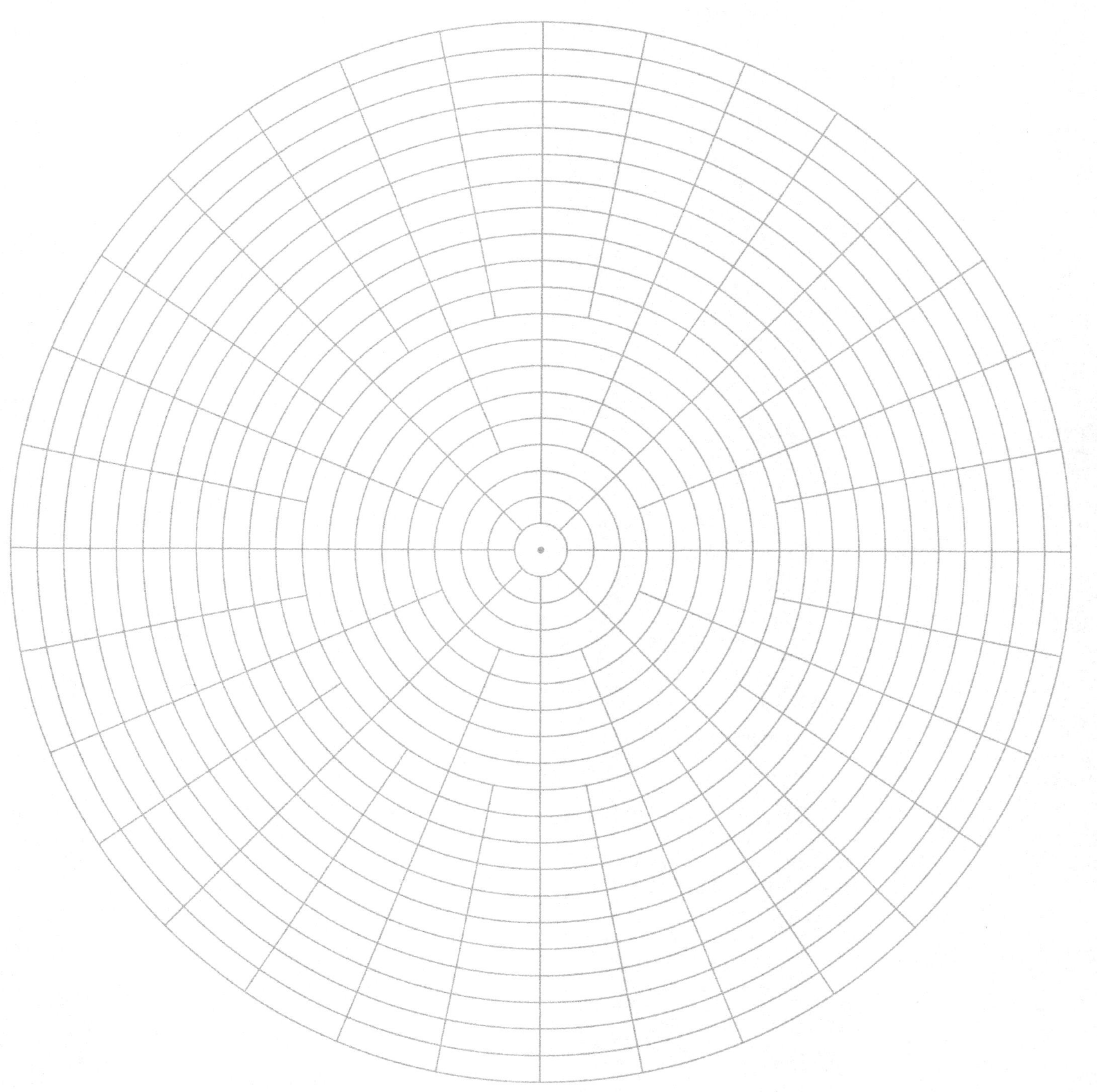

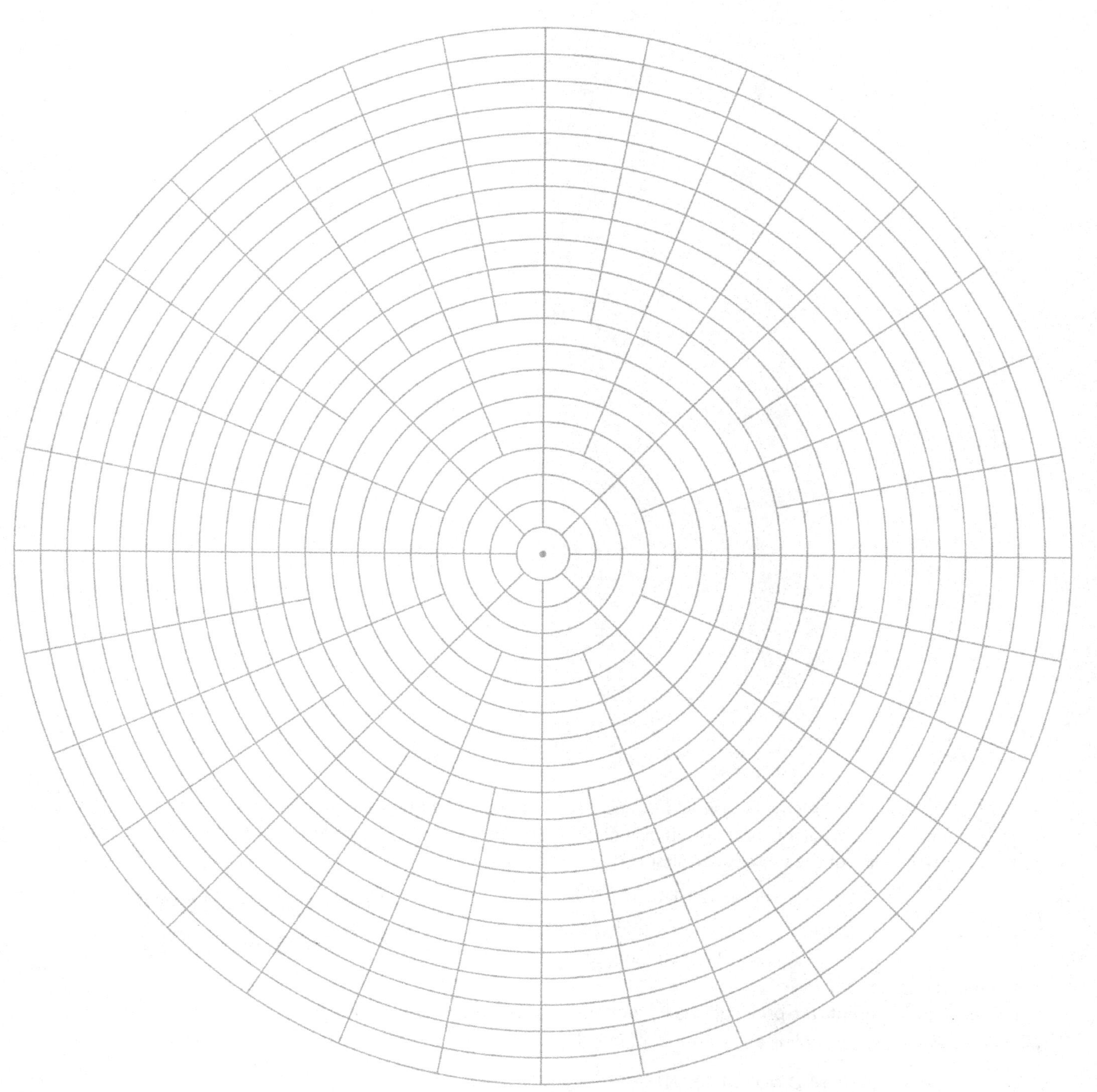

© 2022, Libro Studio LLC. All rights reserved. No part of this publication may be reproduced or transmitted in any form or by any means, electronic or mechanical, including photocopying, recording, or any other information storage and retrieval system, without the written permission of the publisher.

ISBN: 978-1-63578-387-2

Current contact information can be found at:
www.LibroStudioLLC.com

Disclaimers:

This book and its contents are provided "AS IS" without warranty of any kind, expressed or implied, and hereby disclaims all implied warranties, including any warranty of merchantability and warranty of fitness for a particular purpose.

The creator and publisher DO NOT GUARANTEE THE ACCURACY, RELIABILITY, OR COMPLETENESS OF THE CONTENT OF THIS BOOK OR RELATED RESOURSES AND IS NOT RESPONSIBLE FOR ANY ERRORS OR OMISSIONS. We apologize for any inaccurate, outdated, or misleading information. Feel free to contact us if you have questions or concerns.

Made in the USA
Las Vegas, NV
14 December 2023

82873463R00063